The

MW01275623

"The Power of Persisten ... powerful optimism that give readers something they can digest for the rest of their lives"
--Derrick Hayes, Encouragement Speaker

"It can be hard to believe the old adage that persistence can move mountains... until you've read The Power of Persistence!"
--Stephen Balzac, President, 7 Steps Ahead, LLC

"This book, very simply, focuses on a key ingredient to being successful in work and everyday life. It shares insights, personal stories and tips to the most powerful component of success...persistence. Once you fully understand and embrace it's beauty and strength, you can unleash your own personal power. Go for it!!"
--Mary Jones, Host of The Mary Jones Show, Co-host of *All That & More*

The Power of Persistence is a compilation of inspirational stories of people who have refused to be defeated, discouraged, resigned or victimized. Read these compelling stories of courage, commitment, and perseverance and step into your own personal power.
--Dr. Joe Rubino, CEO CenterForPersonalReinvention.com Creator, SelfEsteemSystem.com

"This book is a timely reminder that even the most difficult circumstances can be overcome with determination and positive action."
--John Follis, Entrepreneur

"The Power of Persistence is a wonderfully inspirational collection of stories that will encourage readers to be steadfast in pursuing their dreams. Never give up - you will achieve what you truly desire in life."
   --Jan Malloch, Positive Thinking and Achievement Expert

Dear Justin, I started reading your book and I couldn't put it down... it filled me with emotions of awe and admiration and has inspired me to step up and take my life to the next level. The stories you share in the book prove to me once again how amazing we can be when we put our heart and soul to it! Thank you for creating this gift to humanity!
   --Masha Malka, best-selling author of *The One Minute Coach: change your life one minute at a time*

"Success requires persistence. There is no other way. To keep you on your path toward success, read this book."
   --Elliott Katz, author of *Being the Strong Man A Woman Wants: Timeless wisdom on being a man*

"This book teaches you perhaps the most important success principle ever discovered-- Persistence. When you apply it to your life your life will be forever changed."
   --Joanna Vaiou, Founder of Success Business Mindset

The Power of Persistence reminds each one of us how important it is to love our life enough to stay true to it despite all odds. Never trite, the compliation of stories Justin Sachs has brought to us provides inspiration, humor, and soulful exuberance. Soak them in and treasure every lesson, triumph, and nugget of wisdom--the book is a treasure chest!
   --Beth Wilson, best-selling author, He's Just No Good For You, speaker, and TV Host of In The Sisterhood on Blip.tv

The Power Of Persistence

Real Life Stories of Real People Creating Extraordinary Results

Justin Sachs

Foreword by Mina Watkins

www.MotivationalPress.com

Published by Motivational Press, Inc., 7668 El Camino Real, #104-223, Carlsbad, CA 92009

ISBN: 978-0-9825-7550-5

Compiled by Justin Sachs

www.JSachs.com

Publisher: Motivational Press, Inc
7668 El Camino Real, #104-223
Carlsbad, CA 92009
www.MotivationalPress.com

For information about custom editions, special sales, premium and corporate purchases, please contact Motivational Press Special Sales Department at 888-357-4441.

Dedication

The Power of Persistence is dedicated to you, because it is through your commitment, dedication, and perseverance that we will create the change this world so desperately needs. It is through your power and your possibility that we will unleash a force of transformation throughout the planet and it is because you stood up by picking up this book that together, we can create more, do more, and be more in every area of our lives.

Written in loving memory of Bunnie Sachs, Elsa Kovacs, and Anne Kaye.

Table of Contents

"Twenty years from now you will be more disappointed by the things that you didn't do than by the ones you did do. So throw off the bowlines. Sail away from the safe harbor. Catch the trade winds in your sails. Explore. Dream. Discover"
~ Mark Twain

Acknowledgements

As I began to think of all the people who supported me in completing this book, the list kept growing and growing:

First and foremost, a huge acknowledgement to the authors who's stories have made this book the powerful inspirational it is for people throughout the world.

My mom, dad, Jacob, grandparents, and Uncle Jerry for their unconditional, support, advice, love and guidance. Reggie Batts, one of my greatest role models, for his guidance, support, leadership and generosity. Craig and Rachel Parks, and Corey Rubin for their close friendship, critical analysis, leadership development and overall support. Rabbi David Frank, Rabbi Jeff Brown, and Robin Rubin for their spiritual guidance throughout my life.

Helen Diller for her inspiration, support, and belief in youth leadership. Joel and Heidi Roberts, and Judy Rybak for their media and public relations strategic planning and development. Sarah Van Zanten and Ariel Lawrence for their marketing and promotion expertise, and their hard work and dedication to making this book a success. Lauren Weinberg for her structural support, content development and for her constant friendship. Rachel Kenny for her editorial guidance, marketing advice, and constant support.

My advisory team: Ann McIndoo, Reginald Batts, Christopher J. McCarty, William Savage, Robert Gould, Gene McNaughton, Bernhard Dohrmann, Russell A. Davis, Dr. Barbara Rosenberg, Debbie Ann Schneider, and Patti Coffee.

Special thanks to my mentors and role models whose personalities have most impacted me: Kathy Buckley, Master Ken Church, Mark Victor Hansen, Anthony Robbins, Gary King, Steven Linder, Marlon Smith, Greg Reid.

To my Accomplishment Coaching Family, my closest friends and family for their everlasting love and support.

Foreword by Mina Watkins

The power of one's vision is immeasurable in pushing people through the tough times. It all begins with a vision of what's possible. One can really imagine what their future holds. This is the person who has full conviction that what they want will happen whether or not they know how. Until you have that, you will not see results. In other words, the results will not happen until you believe its possible. It is up to you to trust your vision and do whatever it takes to bring that vision alive. I have found that when I believe something will happen no matter what, it does. It also means that pushing through the difficult times takes a lot of focus on the end prize. If you keep your eyes on the prize, then it will happen. This takes practice, and the one key ingredient is persistence. When a person is living with determination, they live with perseverance in every area of their lives. They will do whatever it takes and stick with the plan to reach their desired goal. When living with perseverance, your actions and visions are broadened. Consider this imagery for a moment. You are in a room, and your body is filled with a vision of possibility. You know that you have something inside of you that is yearning to come out. Maybe you envision something great, where you are a leader and you are collaborating with people to do extraordinary things, such as ending world hunger. Or maybe you are a scientist looking to find the cure for cancer. As you stand there in the room you begin to believe more and more that what you envision is possible. Then the possibility fills up the room and expands outside of the room. It does not stop there. The vision and possibility travels farther and farther out, spreading across the town or city. Then zoom out and imagine it is covering the earth. Zoom out even farther into space, and it is covering the empty space, the stars, and the galaxy until it embodies the universe. Now there is nothing stopping you from finding the cure, or ending world hunger. You are liberated by the energy that pushes you into action. Imagine how you would feel in that moment.

Persistence is liberating when one reaches their goal. You may feel a sense of contentment, or maybe you feel pure joy and satisfaction knowing that you achieved something great. Something miraculous occurs within you. The more you are persistent in one area of life, the hungrier you become for persistence in other areas of your life. Over the years my persistence level has increased dramatically. I've practiced persistence so much that I have *become* persistent. Each time I reach a goal, I reinforce myself to believe that I am capable of anything. The feeling I get is riveting.

When I was a little girl, I received my first bike with training wheels. It was pink with a white wicker basket. It was just perfect! However, no one in my family was available to teach me how to ride the bike. Several years went by and I turned 8 years old. I still had not learned how to ride a bike. I decided that if there was nobody to teach me, then I will teach myself. One day I grabbed my father's wrench and took off the training wheels. At that time, I was living in an apartment complex with my family where there were wide-open spaces for the residents to park. I took my little pink bike that I had outgrown, walked it out into the parking lot, and looked for a small slope. I headed up the slope, stopped to turn the bike downward, and I sat on the seat. I lifted my feet off and slowly began to roll aiming toward the bottom. After several attempts to go down that hill without putting my feet down on the ground, I began to notice that I was able to balance myself longer and longer each time. I became devoted to walking my bike back up the hill, and riding down the hill over and over again. Eventually I put my feet on the pedals, and learned to balance myself without falling to the side. As I felt more confident, I began pedaling. Then I started to continue along on flat pavement gliding easily as I pedaled. I began believing, and I started to have the vision that I would learn how to balance on the bike. My vision was possible the more I persisted to do whatever it took for me to learn how to ride a bike. Who knew that I could learn without first knowing how? It was at that moment when I realized that my persistence paid off. I learned how to ride a bike, and it felt really good knowing that I had accomplished this obstacle. Learning to overcome obstacles gives you extreme power. Hence, the power of persistence.

Over the years, I became better at practicing persistence. Growing up with divorced parents and three other siblings, I knew that college was not possible unless I found a way to pay for my own education. Initially I believed that going to college was not in my plans. At age 18, I graduated high school and went straight into the workforce to earn a living instead of attending college. After a few years earning a comfortable paycheck, I felt something was missing. Going to college and having a degree, I thought, would open up more opportunities. I believed that having a college education was a powerful experience for personal growth. Completing college and graduating would require me to overcome significant obstacles. Not having money to pay for education was one of the biggest obstacles, but it was a challenge I was ready to face. I was doing well working at a large financial firm, but it wasn't enough to live a comfortable life. As much as it was a steady paycheck and there was potential for growth and promotion, it was time for me to move on. I chose to step back as a way to step forward into my future. I went into this decision knowing very well that quitting meant I would be living under limited income and that the challenges I would face would not be easy. However, I was also leaving knowing that whatever my future holds, that I would be taken care of and it was the right choice to make. I did not have much in my savings – only a few months worth to cover expenses and rent. Yet I somehow knew that I would be okay. I had a vision to finish college, and I trusted my vision. I believed in something greater even though I did not know what to expect. During the course of my college years, life happened, and I experienced quite a few bumps in the road.

Life can be challenging at times when there are circumstances that may get in the way. I had a boyfriend that took time away from my studies. There were times I became tired of all the studying, and so I relaxed a few semesters. Despite all of this, I was still determined that I would finish college and I did not lose sight of my goal. I applied for loans and financial aid each semester to help cover monthly rent and expenses. Each time I waited for my check from the aid's office, my bank account was completely dry. Because my parents didn't live sedentary lives, I was forced to live with roommates under harsh conditions. I learned to endure living with someone who had an eating disorder, which affected her interactions with people. Another roommate was clinically diagnosed with multiple personality disorder and as a kleptomaniac. I also lived with a burly Italian man most likely connected to the mafia. This meant that my stress levels were high and had the potential to affect my studies, or even worse leave me wanting to quitting college.

Giving up or quitting was tempting when I had the option to find a full-time position somewhere earning decent income to live without roommates. However, my vision was greater. I chose to endure being locked out when my paranoid roommate changed the locks to the house. I chose to endure living in my father's senior citizen apartments, sneaking in and out without the other residents spotting me so as to avoid the risk of my father losing his home. I chose to sleep in the bathtub night after night, locking myself in the bathroom with the fan on and a wet towel under the doorway to avoid being choked by the chain-smoking roommate. I chose all of this because I was going to finish college no matter what. I managed through all of this because my vision of graduating college was greater than the circumstances that I endured. I was tested multiple times by the circumstances that I faced as all of us are in the pursuit of our dreams. I pushed through the difficult times that required persistence. The day I graduated college was the best moment of my life. It felt gratifying knowing that I was able to overcome the obstacles and accomplish this goal. Looking back, every single experience was worth it, and taught me much more about life.

Individuals encounter different experiences in their lives that dictate the choices. Different experiences may or may not be obstacles to different people. When I mention circumstances, I am referring to events that influence a person's choice or decision. For some, the circumstances may be a spouse or a family member that doesn't share the same vision. Or for some individuals it is the fear of what others may think. Others may feel that their job gets in the way of what they really want in life. Sometimes our vision of what we want is not clear, and our lack of clarity impacts our choices. Yet these life events or circumstances are always going to be there. Whether it is family, children, relationships, work, or what have you, we have our own experiences that may get in the way of what we want. Reflect on this previous thought for a moment. The circumstances will always be there whether or not you want them to be there. So ask yourself, if there will always be circumstances, and if you were to make a choice without having those circumstances in existence, how would your life go? What would you choose? Could it be that you would choose being persistent, doing whatever it takes, pushing through the tough times to get what you want? And would you choose knowing that it would give you great joy and satisfaction when you reach the end prize? If you knew that persistence pays off to have what you ultimately feel is right, would you say yes to those obstacles? Would you allow the circumstances to be in existence and get what you want?

Remember the imagery of a vision of possibility filling up the galaxy earlier? There is something inside of you yearning to come out, and imagine it is greater than you. Imagine how you would feel from the energy. I invite you to practice being persistence. Focus on the end prize, live with perseverance in every area of your life, and watch yourself become hungrier for more. Imagine how much power you will gain from your vision coming alive.

About Mina Watkins
Mina Watkins is a highly trained Transformational Coach and Speaker. Her coaching method is ontologically based, and she is dedicated to working in partnership, giving her clients an open space to fully engage in creating transformations that have lasting effects. She commits herself to her clients' greatness as they continue to produce extraordinary results in all areas of life such as, romantic relationships, career advancement, business growth, finance, health, and well-being. Her prior experiences include sales, marketing, operations, and small business management. She is tenacious and self-taught in many topics including health and nutrition, investments, technology, real estate, and entrepreneurship. She holds a Bachelors Degree in Psychology from California State University, Fullerton. Mina strives to conserve and minimize her carbon footprint, and she takes action in environmental causes as she actively volunteers her time to nonprofit organizations. www.lifecoachminawatkins.com

Introduction

Congratulations on finding *The Power of Persistence*. I'm so excited to be here with you and I'm so excited to share with you the single most important characteristic in shaping your future, and in choosing success. If there's anything I've learned in the past seven years that I've been in the personal development industry it's that there is one characteristic that, above all, creates success among the most extraordinary people. That one characteristic is persistence.

If we look throughout the world in every industry, in every culture, there's one consistent trend among every single successful individual, and that trend is the ability to persevere beyond a shadow of a doubt. It's the ability to stand up beyond everyone else and take a step forward when everyone else sits down.

Before we get started I'd like to take a moment to acknowledge you, because it's not just anyone who would pick up a book called *The Power of Persistence*. It isn't every day that people decide to do what they need to in order to be successful.

Only the most extraordinary individuals, the top minute fragment of a percent who actually step up and take action towards creating success in their lives. Simply by picking up this book, you've chosen to step up and I acknowledge you for taking on that feat.

If we look throughout history at some of the greatest leaders-- Abraham Lincoln, Martin Luther King Jr., Colonel Sanders, Mark Victor Hansen, Steve Jobs -- the most extraordinarily successful people are those who have persisted beyond the norm.

I'll share their stories with you in a moment, but take just a moment now before we get started and consider all of the areas of your life where you could show just a bit more persistence in creating the results you're after. What are the areas where you stand back when you could take that next step forward, the areas where if you just persevere a little bit longer a whole world of possibility will open up for you?

I want to share with you my story of how persistence started in my life. At the age of four I started in Martial Arts and I was, a white belt, as all do when starting out. I was going through the forms and sparring for years and years. I was consistently trying to kick higher and higher, but I was often made fun of because I could only kick waist high.

All the way up until I reached red belt (one step away from black belt) I could only kick slightly above my waist. Bit by bit, moment by moment, over the 10 years I was in Martial Arts I worked hard until finally, one day, I was kicking above my head.

But that's not the only element of persistence that's shown up in my life. Throughout the course of my progression through the belt colors, on my way to becoming a black belt, and later an instructor, I stopped. Not once, not twice, but three times. For a total of three years throughout my journey, I stopped. I took a break, but I never gave up.

When someone has a goal, something they're truly committed to creating, or when they say, "No matter what!" they step up beyond a shadow of a doubt and create that which they imagine in their lives.

When I was 15, I was blessed by the opportunity to walk into an Anthony Robbins seminar and it totally transformed my life. I had heard about the concepts of persistence, perseverance, of creating a vision and actualizing a vision, setting your goals and following through, but never had an experience of implementing them into my life.

When I was 16 years old, I was at my high school and a group of Neo-Nazis called West Coast Destruction were students at my school but also spent a lot of time in the area in which I worked. Day in and day out for a course of two months I was verbally and physically attacked by these Neo-Nazis and I had a choice. I got to choose whether or not I wanted to step up and defy the odds; whether I wanted to stand in the face of that which limited me, that which pushed me down, or whether I wanted to cower down into a small ball and let them get the best of me. I had the choice of pushing forward or giving up. As most of us do in an area of our lives, we have the choice of whether we persist or give up.

So when the bullies confronted me, I knew what it meant to stand up and persist. But not everyone does. And that is why I put this book together: to give people the understanding that persistence is a choice, something we get to create at any given moment. But more importantly, to show that success is a choice.

The truth is that persistence equals success. What I mean by this is that if we look at those who are the most successful in the world, persistence is the common denominator. Persistence is the thing that we've seen in each and every individual who has created the most successful businesses, political careers, relationships, etc.

Those that are losing the most weight – persistence.

Those that stop smoking – persistence.

Everywhere we look we see signs of persistence in those that are creating the most challenging and rewarding results. It is not always natural; it's a learned trait. What this means though, is that success is simply a choice.

If there's one thing I'd like you to take from this book it's that success is a choice and that the one missing piece for you in creating that success for yourself is persistence.

What happened next in my life was just extraordinary: I had gotten my black belt and was teaching Martial Arts, but I felt it was time for me to create something to help others. I chose to begin a nonprofit organization called the Peak Performance Lifestyles Foundation.

I was 16 years old and brought together a group of 12 of my friends from throughout the United States, Canada and the United Kingdom. We came together and created a program that allowed the greatest leaders amongst youth to come together and engage in acts of community service:

To work together to heal the community
To bring people together to care for one another
To love one another
To be of service for one another

It was through this process that we, over the next six months, developed 12 Passionate about Contribution teams in communities throughout the United States, Canada and the United Kingdom.

It was the most extraordinary process for me to see what the act of persistence would create, because there were plenty of things that could have stood in our way. As with all of our projects in life, there are plenty of things to hold us back. We could have stood down and have been unwilling to create change out of the limitations that had been set forth from us.

We were young, all between the ages of 14 and 16, and for us to stand tall and create something as powerful as that, for us to get our 501(c)(3) status to become a registered nonprofit organization in the United States, and for us to then get everything we needed for our projects donated by the communities we worked with...it was a process of persistence like you would not imagine.

The next challenge for me was writing my first book: *Your Mailbox is Full: Real Teens in the Real World.* Along the process of creating my nonprofit organization, I had been working for Tony Robbins, then for Mark Victor Hansen (Co-Founder of *Chicken Soup for the Soul Series*) and I got inspired. So I picked up my pen, wrote two pages, got what's called "writer's block".

I put my pen down for the next two years until I set myself up for success by putting an accountability structure in place and made sure that I would create exactly what I intended to create a published book. I finished my first book at the age of 18, published it and had it become a bestseller within two weeks of its launch. The list goes on and on in the areas of my life in which I have been able to persist to create results.

Let's take a quick look at some of the most extraordinary leaders and how persistence has shaped their lives.

There was once a politician who failed at business at the age of 21. He was defeated in a legislative race at age 22, he failed again at business at age 24, overcame the death of his lover at age 26, had a nervous breakdown at age 27, lost a congressional race at 34 and 36, lost a senatorial race at 45, failed to become vice president at 47, lost a senatorial race at 49 and then finally was elected to President of the United States of America at age 52.

Now imagine, if he had considered any of these past experiences as failures and had allowed that to stop him from moving forward, he would never have become one of the most extraordinary Presidents of the United States, Mr. Abraham Lincoln.

There's a famous story about Thomas Edison: he tried 9,999 times to perfect the light bulb and he couldn't do it. Someone said, "Are you going to have 10,000 failures?" And he responded, "I didn't fail, I just discovered another way <u>not</u> to invent the electric light bulb."

He got to choose how he perceived his previous experiences and whether or not he perceived them as failures.

Mark Victor Hansen, a close friend of mine and an extraordinary mentor and businessman. He is the coauthor of *Chicken Soup for the Soul Series* that has now sold over 144 million copies in over 20 languages worldwide.

But did you know that over 110 publishers, in their pursuit to be published, turned down Mark Victor Hansen and Jack Canfield? They went to New York, and it wasn't until a publisher's wife got a hold of the manuscript and all night long she was waking her husband saying "Look at this, look at this" Finally the publisher agreed to publish it.

Now here's a story about another individual. His name was Colonel Sanders, the founder of Kentucky Fried Chicken. He was a military retiree and had nothing to his name, except his mother's chicken recipe. So what did he do? He took his old sports wagon out and began driving to restaurant after restaurant after restaurant.

His intention was to sell the chicken recipe, but he was turned down time and time again he was turned down; 1,007 times before he received his first yes and that one yes is what made possible Kentucky Fried Chicken possible.

The last individual I want to tell you about is Steve Jobs, the President and founder of Apple Computer. Members of his own board of directors kicked him out of his own company. He could have allowed this to stop him, but instead he stood up. It was only because he persisted that he was voted back in as Chairman of Apple. He created the iPod, the iPhone and a new line of Mac Computers. Had he not, we probably would not have ever experienced an iPod or an iPhone.

As you can see the stories go on and on of the most extraordinary individuals creating powerful results, as a direct reflection of their persistence. Because time and time again, individuals are stopped along their journey. Just because they're stopped, it doesn't mean that they are failures or that their project will never work. It simply means that they're one step closer to achieving the result that they desire.

I want to take a moment to thank you for choosing to read *The Power of Persistence*. I'm so excited to have you with me, and I am so excited to begin this journey with you.

I know that you're going to learn so much, as I have, from the individuals who have shared their stories with you. They are some of the most incredible people you'll ever hear from and they're some of my closest friends.

I can't wait to hear about the influence this book will have on your life.

"Nothing in the world can take the place of persistence. Talent will not; nothing is more common than unsuccessful men with talent. Genius will not; unrewarded genius is almost a proverb. Education will not; the world is full of educated derelicts. Persistence and determination alone are omnipotent."
~Calvin Coolidge

"The reasonable man adapts himself to the world; the unreasonable one persists in trying to adapt the world to himself. Therefore all progress depends on the unreasonable man."
~ **George Bernard Shaw**

One Step at a Time By Ann McIndoo, Author's Coach

"Persistence is like mowing the lawn, one blade at a time."
-Ann McIndoo, Author's Coach

Whatever it is you desire, there is always a strategy, tool or resource to get it. Whether your desire is business or personal, persistence is one of the most powerful tools you can use to get what you wish for. When I look at the wins and victories I have enjoyed, persistence always comes up as one of the most effective tools I have used to achieve success.

What is persistence? I learned through both success and failure that persistence is to keep moving forward, no matter what, until you reach your goal or achieve your outcome. *Persistence means not letting anything deter you from your quest.* Do not let distractions in the form of other people and their agendas, low priority or unrelated items, other personal or business matters, interrupt, cause doubt or stop you. You must keep moving forward, even if it is just one small step. Remember the old proverb, a journey of 1,000 miles begins with one step? Take one step, then another, then another, this will create momentum. The importance of momentum is critical. As long as you have momentum, and persist, there is no stopping you.

What does the Power of Persistence give you? A plan of action, steps to keep moving forward, a goal to work on, a huge victory or reward when you persist to success. I have always begun a project with 3 things in mind:

- Knowing my outcome;
- Having a plan to implement; and
- Taking massive and consistent action.

How do I use my persistence? The key is to decide what you want so the act of persisting to achieve your goal is a normal course of action. Once you decide what you want, you can create a plan to implement it and begin your consistent action to reach your goal, *then you can actually **be persistent.*** Being persistent, not giving up or letting anything deter you, is a critical component to being successful.

The Magic of Persistence is everywhere. Persistence has been a powerful strategy for me, especially in business. Using persistence, I have:

- Achieved many of my goals.
- Kept moving forward toward obtaining a goal or completing a goal, even when I wanted to stop or give up. My powerful friend, persistence, kept me going.
- Solved a problem, dilemma, or challenge.
- Taken advantage of an opportunity.
- Stayed strong in a leadership role.
- Enjoyed the victory!

There are many benefits to being persistent, especially if you know what you want and where you are going.

One of my biggest victories has been starting an industry trend. In the 1980's when personal computers were being introduced, I started a company called Computer Training Services. I began teaching people how to use computers. No one else was doing it at that time. I didn't let it stop me. I saw a need and I filled it. I made a plan, took action and became the first and largest computer training company in the United States. I taught over 15,000 people how to use a PC. It was very lucrative.

Another huge win and personal favorite has been becoming a successful Author's Coach. When I started my business, there were lots of people who gave me a polite nod, or a quizzical look when I told them what I did. I did not let their doubt stop me. I kept writing, creating, taking steps on my action plan and building my business, one step at a time. The result?

- A fun and profitable business that allows me to create and have the lifestyle I desire.
- I have helped authors produce more than 250 books since January of 2005.
- I have helped dozens of people make their book-writing dream come true.
- I have helped make a difference by getting books out into the world.
- Most importantly, I enjoy what I do and I am living my passion.

What is my Power of Persistence strategy? What is my winning formula? Here's what I do to persist:
- Decide what my goal or desire is in great detail. I think it, visualize it, write it down, describe it out loud, share it with a couple of people to get feedback and input. Read your formula for success every day and see it, believe it.
- Create an Action Plan – a step-by-step action list of what I need to do to make it happen.
- Take massive actions. First SCHEDULE your steps and then TAKE them! Mark your calendar as to when you are going to complete each step.
- Don't give up – keep doing it! No matter what, as long as your goal is the same, keep moving forward.
- Check your results. Are your action steps getting you closer to what you want? If so, keep doing it. If not:

- Change your approach. See what's working and what needs to be improved. Make the changes and take another step.
- Keep moving forward. See the win, feel the victory. Imagine what life is going to be like when you reach your goal.

How do you get persistence in your life? Create it for yourself – decide that you will take action to meet your goals. I have found that I can only be persistent about something I truly care about or really want. That's why it is important to decide what it is you want. Do you want to be persistent? Decide to be!

How do you make sure your persistence doesn't waiver or you don't lose it? See the win, every day, and keep it alive. Take a step toward your victory every day and reward yourself for each landmark you reach on your journey toward your goal.

Many years ago, I learned the lesson and value of persistence when I decided I wanted to get a puppy. I went to the local animal shelter to get my new pet. I began walking up and down the rows of cages with dogs of all shapes, colors and sizes barking and jumping all over each other to get my attention. As I went down row after row looking for my special dog, not only were there hundreds of dogs to choose from, but 20, 30, 40 rows of dog cages to walk through. I was becoming overwhelmed from the huge lot to choose from and I soon realized I was also very tired from walking on the cold concrete.

As I reached the end of the 40th row, and had not seen the dog that I knew I should take home, I was tired, thirsty and saddened that I had not found my puppy. I wanted to go home with my dog that day. As I reached the end of the last row, disappointed that I had not found my new dog, I saw an employee and asked if there were any more dogs. She gave me that "haven't you seen enough" look, and pointed to a little enclosure about 150 feet away. It looked so far away, but I really wanted my dog so I trudged over to the enclosure to see what was there. There were 5 cages and it was pretty quiet. I walked to the first cage and it was empty! The second cage – empty, third cage, empty. Finally, I reached the fourth cage, empty! There were no dogs here! I must have misunderstood the employee's directions.

I turned around and began walking back to the lobby when I remembered my promise to myself, **I would find my dog today**. I turned around again and walked back to the fifth cage. I glanced in and saw nothing. Then I made myself walk all the way to the end of the cage and they're, in the corner, all curled up in a tight little ball, was a little black and white puppy. There was no jumping, no whining, just two sad little eyes looking up at me. When I tapped on the cage and said, "Hey, little puppy", the puppy wagged the tip of its long tale and I instantly knew this dog was mine.
As it turned out, the puppy was going to be put down that evening and had less than a couple of hours to live. I had saved her life. I took Megan home with me that day. I had her for 14 wonderful years and she was the best dog I ever had. My persistence had paid off.

Persist and your dreams will come true. Reward yourself for each step you take, and remember to enjoy the journey.

About Ann McIndoo
Ann McIndoo is the Author, Write Your Book! And has supported hundreds of authors in getting their books out of

their heads, onto paper, and into the world. Find out more about Ann McIndoo at: www.SoYouWantToWrite.com or email her at Ann@SoYouWantToWrite.com.

From Ruins to Riches: A Modern Greek *Triumph* over *Tragedy* by Christina Andrews

Paralysis, Pins and Needles

I was born in Greece and lived my life like most other normal children, until the age of five when I became paralyzed. I simply woke up one morning and couldn't walk.

I spent the next few months in hospital undergoing a battery of tests; no one knew what the cause of my paralysis was. I was given hundreds of injections.

Tonic

When not being pricked like a human pincushion, I encouraged the other sick kids to get better so that we could all play together. The nurses saw me as a 'tonic' for the other kids and would wheel me all over the children's wards spreading good humor and encouragement with my natural ebullience.

Home

I was eventually allowed to go home and had a nurse that would visit me daily to give me injections and check up on me.

I eventually started to walk again and ran around a lot; I had a lot of time to make up!

I started school and loved it. I was an "A" student who would do everything right. I was a "goody-goody".

Filthy Rich Australia

When I was 8 years old, my dad's cousin who lived in Australia, told him that he was 'filthy' rich and that he should be in Australia not in Greece. Dad had also heard that you could find money *everywhere*; so we packed up everything and came to Australia.

Reality Bites

Once we arrived, needless to say, life wasn't quite what they expected; money wasn't *everywhere*. We were forced to rent one bedroom in a house where we all lived and slept together. We shared the kitchen, the lounge, the bathroom and the yard with the owners.

Mum went from being a happy housewife in our Greek village to working long hours in an assembly line factory. Dad went from having a good government office job to also working in a soulless factory.

Understandably, this was a shock to their system and it took a long time to recover.

In the first two years we kept moving houses and schools. There was no stability and we all pined for our 'good, simple life' back in Greece.

Finally we moved to a house in Prahran and to a new school, the first where we stayed for more than three months! None of us could speak any English and so needed to attend special classes. There was a stigma being a 'Wog' – a 'new' Australian, with our funny accents and strange food.

Star Student

In spite of all this I adapted well and thrived at school, becoming house captain in grade six - a huge achievement, given my inauspicious start to Australia. However hardship was never far away.

In my fourth grade year, my father had an accident at the factory and was unable to work and earn an income. We lived on my mother's salary – a paltry $28 a week. The years passed and through scrimping and saving we were able to buy a small house close to the beach in Melbourne. By now I am in my teens and an early maturing, attractive Greek girl and a worry for my overly protective Greek father.

Marriage at 18

I joined various clubs including a dancing club, where I met my future husband at the age of 15. I married Paul at 18 so that I could move out of my home, as my father was very strict. I really wanted to go clubbing like my other friends did.

It was expected of me to marry at a young age so that I didn't remain 'on the shelf'.

I went to University as a married woman and in my final year of my teaching degree I fell pregnant with my first child. I was also teaching and working on weekends at the same time. Like many migrant families we were keen to start a business and make some *real* money.

Business Birth

In December 1983, we bought our first business, a video library. I worked seven days a week and always took Peita, my baby, to work.

I hired a schoolgirl for a couple of hours a day to take Peita for a walk and to give me a break.

My husband, who worked as an engineer, would relieve me from the shop at seven at night so I could go home and put our baby to bed.

I did this for six months and decided to ask my mum to stop her work so she could look after the baby. It was a full life, but we were building a business and were becoming very good at it.

Booming Business

Over the next few years we opened another five stores and had two more children.

Things were great at that time. Both my husband and I where running the businesses and the money was rolling in. Unfortunately we didn't have the training nor the wisdom to make our money work for us, though we thought it would never run out.

In fact things were going so well that we sold our business to an overseas company and my husband became the managing director of that subsidiary company.

Now the 'real' money would roll in, or so we thought. A rude shock awaited that would change my life forever.

Boom 'Crash'

In the early 1990's we had the economic 'crash'. One of the banking organizations in Perth, Australia went under, and took down the American company we had sold our video stores to.

Although we had 'sold' our business for millions of dollars, we hadn't received all our money, so we tried to take our stores back but to no avail; the authorities went after my husband as the director of this new company - the other director was in the United States and unreachable.

We lost absolutely everything; we went from being multi-millionaires to having nothing to our name overnight. In fact the sheriff and I became best friends at the time, that's how often he visited my house looking for assets to reclaim.

During this stressful time I became pregnant (on the pill) to our fourth child.

This was exciting and painful at the same time, as we didn't have enough food nor money to survive, let alone support another child.

But then Dean arrived, the only boy among three girls. We have always been eternally grateful.

By now though we were desperate for income to support our family of six. I went back to teaching and my husband tried a couple of failed attempts at other businesses, because by this time my husband felt like a failure and wasn't able to get things working as he used to. It also didn't help that our so-called 'friends' deserted us.

From Good to Bad to Worse

When we had money in abundance - the mansion, fast cars and so on, our house was like a railway station at peak hour; people were in and out constantly; we were always very generous entertainers. When we lost everything there were only a couple of people who encouraged and supported us. It was enough to cause a nervous breakdown, which I had. There seemed no way out.

But, with the grace of God I found the strength to be able to get up and continue with life.

A Ray of Light and my Strengths Shine Through

I started work in the telecommunications industry and quickly realized there was huge potential for developing a business. I was proved correct and the business, which I started then, remains highly successful today.

During this time I recognized that I had potential but that it was untapped, so I embarked on a steep personal development trajectory, attending any course I felt would improve me. I was determined to change my life, no matter what it took.

I also met a business associate who took me under his wing and believed in me and my ability and drove me towards my passion at all times.

The message I received loud and clear was that it doesn't matter how many times you fall, what matters is how many times you got back up.

Still Challenges despite Success

Life was still not easy. We had lost millions of dollars and I had the wind taken out of my sails and yet despite all odds I got back up and kept going regardless of what everyone thought. I also became confident in my abilities and became very astute at business.

My husband at this stage went to work overseas and has lived there for the majority of the time. I was left to bring up four children on my own, which I did and ran two businesses on my own. My husband and I eventually separated, though he remains in their life.

My life has since been balancing family and business. It's been tough, but rewarding.

The setbacks have made me more resilient.

No Excuses

What is your excuse? Who knocked the wind out of your sails? Have you had the guts to get up and go one more time? Or are you allowing your circumstances to keep you where you are? What are you afraid of? Failure? But what if you succeed? How will you ever know?

It's a Risk. Take it!

Did I have to take risks? You bet! I risked my children growing up and being 'drop outs' in society. I risked loosing the money I didn't have. I could have kept going with teaching and receiving a salary, but that wasn't good enough for me. I've always believed that my children and I deserve the best that life has to offer. I didn't want to live a mediocre life. I didn't want to just get through week-to-week or month-to-month. I took a chance. I have the most beautiful and well-balanced children you could ever meet. I have extremely successful businesses and I am always adding new adventures and businesses to my bow.

Goal Driven & Passionate

Through my many challenges I learnt some very valuable skills. One of them is to write down my goals and date them. To this day at the beginning of every year I write down my goals and get great enjoyment through out the year going back and ticking off each one that I have achieved, even though at the time I wrote them, they seemed impossible.

I still have goals, dreams and aspirations of what I want to do next and what I want to achieve. I am still planning and taking risks on a daily basis, but I would rather be alive and feel the passion and the adrenalin of what I love to do than wallow in my circumstances and become complacent.

My children and I have a great life. We travel together, explore different places and cultures, spend as much time as we can together as a family but at the same time we are all individuals each one of us pursuing our own dreams and aspirations.

Your Gift

What better gift can you give your children than to teach them by example to follow their dreams and not allow circumstances get in the way?

My suggestion to you is that you find some one who you can look up to, hold on to their coat tails and go for it. If you have a burning desire and a passion to do something in your life don't let anybody steal your dream. Definitely do not allow your circumstances keep you stuck where you are at the moment. "Get off your butt and do something". Make something of your life! Let the fire burn in your eyes and let your passion drive you.

To create wealth all you need is a WHY. The reason cannot be money; it has to be <u>what</u> money will get for you.

So, find a purpose, a passion and drive and you will have a winning formula. Never ever forget to keep getting up if you get knocked down.

Enjoy the journey!

About Christina Andrews

Christina Andrews' life has been all about persistence; overcoming physical, personal and financial challenges – from childhood paralysis in Greece, to relocating to Australia, and later, as a single mother with four children under ten.
Now a successful telecommunications entrepreneur, property investor and founder of an online university for single parents, she inspires other women to become **CATS; -** make courageous **C**hoices, have a positive mental **A**ttitude and **T**ake Opportunities when they appear. Christina lives in Melbourne, Australia.

The Parking Space for Dreams By Karen V. Kibler

We like to have results <u>now</u>. We are a society of instant results, and we have forgotten that goals often require patience and steadfast progress. It can be frustrating and tests our patience. But if we are really lucky, we come to appreciate that there are hidden blessings in the waiting.

My goal was to write a book about my experiences with clinical depression. For many years, one of my sisters had been urging me to write my story, and she was fairly persistent in her encouragement. It was finally just simpler to give in and do as she suggested rather than to resist all that encouragement. So, here I was, all set and ready to get that book on the shelves of bookstores.

All those who have published a book of any kind can predict what happened next. My world of instant results had not prepared me in any way for the process ahead of me. My goal was a worthy one, no question. My motives in tackling the task were of good quality. My qualifications were not outstanding, but they were sufficient. So, how hard could this be? I had already survived substantial obstacles in my life: I had recovered from two battles with clinical depression, one resulting from a divorce and one from the death of my second husband; I had been a single parent most of my life; I had completed graduate school to earn a Ph.D. past the age of forty; I had bravely risked a third marriage. All these obstacles were conquered only through effort, commitment, and perseverance. This was but another challenge that surely could not be any more difficult than those I had already met. Someone once told me about a friend who was convinced she could concentrate on a parking place being available where she wanted to park, and it always materialized. I've tried that a number of times without success; my theory is that positive thinking must be accompanied by tangible effort. Positive thinking alone may not always provide a parking space, but it makes the search so much more promising.

My search began with a "small" step: write the story. A hundred authors will probably describe a hundred methods for initiating the task of writing: an outline, random ideas jotted down, possible plot themes, character development, chapter titles, time lines, etc. As a first time author I tried several methods, and I did eventually find one that got me started: several pages of a manuscript finally appeared. The story had begun.

Through the following months I found that there were all sorts of diversions that could slowed my progress. Memories of long ago had to be corroborated with facts, such as accurate dates and places and the research took time. Decisions had to be made about the content: where did truth become unnecessary embellishment? Could events potentially hurtful to others in the telling be omitted or altered to be less hurtful? Some of the decisions were not easy to resolve, and I allowed weeks to pass with no solution until finally the drive to continue overcame the fear of choosing incorrectly. As difficult as the writing was – nothing slowed me down as successfully as the fear of failure. The questions battered me constantly. What if no one wanted to read this book? What if my family was embarrassed by it? What would people think of me if they did read it? Might it not be better if it was left a private manuscript? Then no one would need to judge it, and no one would laugh at me or scorn my attempt.
But that parking place would just simply not relinquish its allure. I wanted to park this book.

With optimism freshly in bloom, I finished the first draft and stepped into the next part of the venture: pitching the book to an agent.

I still remember where I was sitting many years ago when I first used the internet. Today we take it for granted, and there is no topic that is not instantly accessible. Having information at my fingertips today meant I could easily search online for a book agent. Of course, what I discovered is that there were hundreds of them. I could narrow the field by identifying my book genre, but first I had to be capable of identifying my genre. Then there was the question of agents that will take new clients or not; agents that will accept manuscripts by email or require hard copies by regular mail; agents that want query letters only or those that want book proposals. Once I figured out the answers to all those questions, I was still left with how to choose among the ones caught in my criteria filter. Should I base it on gender? The agent's geographical location? Web page design?

I was so naive. Even though numerous websites warn new authors to expect countless rejections, I was still unprepared for the overwhelming number of rejections I received! There are many "how to get published" websites and most of them are excellent. I got invaluable advice from many that I studied, and every one of them warned that it would require a thick skin and unprecedented perseverance to get my book published. Unfortunately for me, the one category of website I had not yet discovered was the one of watch groups who warn of shysters out there, just waiting to grab your manuscript, pick your pocket, and take your book nowhere. After all the rejections, the first email I got from someone who was interested in representing me was naturally a cause for jubilation! Never did I question the legitimacy of the agency. When the representative told me they were excited about my book, I marveled at their good taste. When I was told that the goal was to quickly get a contract signed and move forward I was certain they would quickly place my book in bookstores across the country. When I was asked to hire a recommended editing firm to make the manuscript publisher-ready, I thought I had moved into the big leagues. When I read on the agency's website that they represented more than 10,000 books, I was very impressed with myself for being chosen. Not until the day that I asked the representative during a telephone conversation how many of the 10,000 books the agency represented were now published and was told that there were *nine* did I finally start to see the picture. Yes, the agency was a fraud. These people were not likely to even get the book presented to a publisher's staff. They were only going to share the profits from the editing firm, while tying up the rights to my book. They offered a contract to every single author who contacted them – there was no choosing of only the best ones. They deliberately planted hope and joy in hearts while having no plans or intentions of getting anyone's book published. They were in the business of promising soaring while delivering only devastation. I was stunned at how much it hurt.

Months passed with no more attempts to pursue an agent or publisher. My life was busy and I didn't need any further disappointments. The parking place could go to someone else.

I finally realized I had just been in the wrong parking garage. It took a long time, but the voice telling me there was still a parking place with my name on it slowly became audible once again insisting that I could do this.
And with that final urging, I started on a path that wound around a bit, was sprinkled with luck and possibly with a miracle or two, and led to Wyatt-MacKenzie Publishing. My book was published just a year after I had given up all hope of continuing my pursuit.

And those hidden blessings? For more than 25 years I have wished I could thank the author of *The Cracker Factory*. Reading that book is probably what saved me later when I had plunged into my second chasm of depression; the book definitely had a profound impact on my life. All these years later, as my book neared its publication date, I not only had an opportunity to thank Joyce Rebeta-Burditt for writing her book that had helped me so much – she even graciously agreed to write the foreword for my book. Her friendship is indeed a blessing I would never have received had I not pursued the parking space.

The book isn't a bestseller, but it has touched lives, which was the purpose of writing the book. It is there now, available to keep the circle of healing going, which is the reason a parking place was needed. And a dream nearly abandoned has instead inspired new dreams.

About Karen Kibler

Karen Kibler was raised in the small farming community in Iowa. She earned her Bachelor's Degree from the University of Iowa in 1977, and soon after relocated to Arizona. She received a Ph.D. in 1997 from Arizona State University where she is now an Assistant Research Professor and the university Biosafety Manager. The focus of her current research is HIV vaccines and treatments. Prior to her career in science she held several positions in business, from receptionist to owner, though her resume also includes skills such as welding and heavy equipment operation.

Writing has been a long-time passion of hers; however, until the completion of *The Second Chasm*, her audience was restricted to family and college class professors.

My Practice Wife by Keith Leon

I remember when I met my first wife (I like to call her my practice wife) it felt as if the stars had aligned. We shared things with each other we'd never shared with anyone before. We related so well to each other because we had so much in common. She soon became by best friend in the world.

At first, we let every argument, disagreement or mistake go on by. We loved each other so much and to others we looked like the perfect couple. Unfortunately, we came from homes with divorced parents and grew up with mothers who weren't equipped to raise us. We grew up with dysfunction, poor communication, poverty and verbal abuse as our example of what family looked like. We both carried these behaviors into our marriage.

After the newness of the relationship had worn off, problems started to immerge. I felt like there was always something wrong with me as far as my wife was concerned. She would express the *newest thing* that was wrong with me; I would do my best to change it. Before I knew it, something else would be wrong with me...and so on, and so on, and so on.

There was one major problem; these fights were eating us alive one at a time. Once something is said it can never be unsaid. No amount of "I'm so sorrys" can undo what was said in the heat of the moment. All the verbally abusive statements we were slinging were adding up and chipping away at our self-esteem. We were slowly tearing our relationship apart and didn't even realize it. Even though we loved each other, we didn't have a form of communication that worked. Our communication was horrible at best. After years of this, we decided it was time to part ways.

"The problem is not that there are problems. The problem is expecting otherwise and thinking that having problems is a problem."
~ Theodore Rubin

Losing my best friend, mate, snuggle buddy and wife hurt like nothing I had ever experienced before. Finding my bed empty every morning and night was something that took a very long time to get used to. This *seemed* to be the worst thing that ever happened to me in my life. Believe me, I had some pretty horrible things happen in my life growing up, but this trumped all of them, hands down.

After the pain started to subside a bit, someone told me about a book called, *Men Are From Mars Women Are From Venus*. It was a man who told me about the book, so I picked up a copy. This book enlightened me. I found out that all the things I thought were so strange about me were actually things that most men experienced too. I started to get answers to my question, "Why do women act like that?" And even though I don't think it's ever stated in the book, the message I was getting was that I needed to look at my part of why my former marriage didn't work instead of blaming it all on my ex.

I started doing an inner search and identifying all the ways I had added to our dysfunction. I realized that I was very verbally abusive and didn't communicate well at all because I didn't know how to speak to a woman. I didn't know why she thought certain ways about certain things, and I wasn't really listening to find out the answers.

After I identified the things I needed to work on, I started doing just that. I started to try new forms of communicating with my female boss and co-worker at work. I started to love myself more and forgave myself for judging myself as a bad person. I started being more honest with others and myself and I started to feel a little better each day.

I soon decided to start dating again, and using the Law of Attraction I found my perfect mate. I had made a list of everything that I wanted in my next mate. I included all of the qualities she would posses and I even went on to list physical qualities. I wanted to make sure that I would recognize her as soon as I saw her and know that she was the one I had dreamed up. I realized that I needed to become all of the qualities I wanted to attract so I went to work.

When Maura and I first met, I knew she was the one that I had created in my mind. She fit my list to the letter. She had done a similar process to what I did and had put her list away. When we pulled her list out and read it, I could swear that she had followed me around taking notes because her list described me perfectly inside and out!

We had both come from relationships that were filled with dysfunction and poor communication. We vowed that we would change this pattern and be honest and loving at all times in our communication. We agreed that we would *never* do name calling, as we both saw it as inexcusable.

Together we developed a communication skill called, *The Format.* It is a tool that we both use to this day and have taught it to thousands of people over our years together as relationship experts. The Format is such a great tool that John Gray (author of, *Men Are From Mars Women Are From Venus*) put his endorsement on the front cover of our first book. It was an honor to have his endorsement of our work, because his book had been so instrumental in my self-discovery and how I wanted to do relationship moving forward in my life.

I have been with my wife Maura for ten years now, and it has been the best ten years of my life. Sure we have disagreements. Yes, we fight about stupid things just like everyone else, but we use *The Format* to get the bottom of what is really going on and find a resolution. We went from communication failures to communication experts. We set an intention and we achieved it together.

The worst thing that ever happened to me in my life (my divorce) cleared the way for the best thing that ever happened in my life (my marriage to Maura). We have developed the type of relationship we had always wanted to be in. We're talking about the type of relationship that *adds* to our already great life. One that is built on a foundation of, we are both good enough just the way we are, so there's nothing for us to change or fix about each other.

If someone had told me right after my divorce that it would end up being the best thing that ever happened to me, I would have thought they were crazy. But it has ended up being the truth. I bless my time with my practice wife, as it taught me so much about who I didn't want to be in relationship. Also, it brought forth the best son anyone could ever wish for. I am still good friends with my ex and we are grateful for the time we had together and for the years of friendship to come.

About Keith Leon
Keith Leon is known as "The Singing Trainer." He's an entrepreneur, a family man and a full-time student of life. With his wife Maura, Keith co-authored the best selling book, The Seven Steps to Successful Relationships, acclaimed by best-selling authors, John Gray and Terry Cole Whittaker, and recently Keith has released a book called, Who Do You Think

You Are? Discover The Purpose Of Your Life, with a foreword by Chicken Soup for The Soul's Jack Canfield.

About Keith Leon
Keith is a recognized speaker, mentor, a gifted professional singer and a songwriter. He's spoken at events that included Jack Canfield, John Demartini, Marianne Williamson, Barbara De Angeles and John Gray just to name a few. As a gifted and accomplished vocal soloist and musician, he's performed alongside such musical talents as Ben Verene, Nancy Wilson, Bird York, Carl Anderson and Stevie Wonder. You can learn more about Keith by visiting www.RelationshipMasters.com or www.KeithLeon.com

You Hold the Power – *Believe by Leyla Hur*

*"Keep on believing
And your dreams will come true"*

When I look back over the course of my life I can see many occasions where I have been persistent in achieving a certain goal or desire. I can literally see where persistence paid off and where, if I *had* been persistent, I could have achieved what I had wanted; however, at those times, I did not keep my focus and I ended up losing out on getting what I wanted.

One of the biggest lessons I had in persistence occurred in 2002; I had been misdiagnosed a couple of years previously and had been given massive amounts of medications. I became incredibly sick, suffered a seizure, and my heart stopped; I was resuscitated, incubated, and was in a coma on life support.

When I came out of the coma and was released from the hospital, I could not walk (without assistance), talk, read, write, or function as a normal person would. My brain suffered in a way that was akin to having had a stroke.

At that time, I was given the diagnosis of having residual brain damage with no hope of a cure.

When I received that diagnosis, my whole world stopped. I was 29 years old and I felt like my life was over.

I cried for 20 minutes, and then clarity set in.

I saw that I was at a crossroad in my life. I could continue walking the path that I was on, go home and seek out a "good hobby" that would keep me occupied for the rest of my life, as had been suggested by the doctor;

OR...

I could choose to fight back and begin my journey on a new path.

I made the conscious choice to take the road less travelled, and so I began my biggest journey of persistence and perseverance.

I was a 29-year old woman; fully-grown, and I could not do the things that many of us take for granted. Though I could not walk, talk, read, or write, my brain was cognitive. I still tried to communicate even though others did not understand it. I could not do simple things like hold a knife or a fork, when using a spoon the food went flying over my shoulder much to the chagrin of those seated at tables behind me in a restaurant.

But even with all those dis-advantages, I knew that I had the power within myself to create a positive and incredible change.

When I had been diagnosed with having residual brain damage, I was not given the option of an occupational therapist; not only did the doctor not refer one (a requirement for me to be able to see one), but my provincial health insurance would not pay for me to see one. So I knew that if I wanted to recoup, I would have to do it on my own, and I would have to be persistent within myself once I started, and persevere until I accomplished the end desire that I had set out in my mind.

At this time, I was staying at my parent's home in a bedroom in their basement, and I was not sleeping nights. What better time than at night when the rest of the house was asleep than to work on my recuperation.

The first task I set out to achieve was walking. I knew that to be the independent person I desired to be, I had to be able to move about on my own two feet. I still had my feet, and while I could not feel them, I knew that if I still had them, I *would* make them work.

Creative visualisation is a very powerful thing. I would go into meditation and I would SEE myself walking; I would SEE myself running. I saw myself as I wanted to be. Once I had that visual in my mind, I would affirm it out loud by saying "I walk unaided on both my feet".

Now I had to take an action to take the visual out of my mind and turn it into a reality.

> "There is no passion to be found in playing small – in settling for a life that is less than what you are capable of living."
> ~ Nelson Mandela

The best way was to go to the bathroom. The first few times I went to the bathroom took an enormous amount of time. I literally had to drag myself across my bedroom floor, into the hallway, and into the bathroom. Once in there, I had a brand new challenge... getting up off the floor and onto the toilet. No easy feat, believe me.

The first few times it took *so* long for my journey to and from the bathroom, that by the time I made it back to my bed, I had to turn around and go again!

But I did not give up. It took a few frustrating tries, but I kept going. Even when it got difficult, such as lying on the bathroom floor looking up at the toilet, with a full bladder and having no idea how I was going to hoist myself up. It would have been easy to simply give up, mess myself and wait for someone to come and clean me in the morning. But my determination and desire was so intense that I *refused* to give up.

My persistence payed off when one morning, I got myself out of bed, went up the basement stairs and was sitting and waiting at the breakfast table for my parents. That accomplishment only fuelled me on to regain the other things I was lacking. I now had a formula that worked.

After 45-days, I had relearned to walk, use a pen and write, which lead to my being able to hold and use a fork and a knife, and keep the food in *my* area. Relearning to read was actually the easiest; I simply had to re-teach myself the alphabet and bring it all together. I learned that when our minds expand, they cannot retract.

The most challenging was getting my speech back; not just getting it back, but getting it back to the point where I was easily understood.

Most people are very surprised, even amazed, when they hear my story; and those who witnessed it first hand, can only attribute it to a miracle.

It was indeed a miracle; and it's something that we each hold within. When we have an intense desire to achieve or accomplish something, it is so important to hold that focus, keep that focus, and then take the action steps to achieving that desire and goal.

We must figure out how important is this goal? Why do we want to accomplish it? What kind of blocks would it take to *prevent* us from reaching that goal?

If our desire is strong enough, there will be *nothing* and *no one* who can ever prevent us from reaching our finish line; but what we must determine is *how badly do we want it?*

Once we have it set in our mind what we want, the next step is to visualise already having it. Our minds are so vast; if it can "cure" a diagnosis that was a life sentence, imagine everything else we can achieve. The biggest thing we each have to know, and keep reminding ourselves is this; we already *HAVE* all that we desire; it is simply a matter of opening ourselves up to receive it.

I *knew* that my body was complete and whole, even if I could not feel a large percent of it; it was only a matter of *believing* and then taking the *action steps* to get those parts of me working again. Once I had that down, everything else fell into place. For the things that I had lost, I released with blessing and love, and moved forward knowing that a vacuum had been created for a new blessing to enter.

There is a saying my former modelling agent used to tell me; "Fake it until you make it", well in some situations, that may be what you have to do. For me, I had to "fake" feeling my feet under me, and learn how to walk, how to place my feet on the ground to get walking. Now here is the thing, even though I was walking within a short time, I still could not *feel* my feet, and that took considerably longer to achieve. But eventually, the feeling returned, and the body that I saw myself living in, is now complete.

Over the years, I have achieved so much and it has been because I had a desire in my head and a burning in my heart, plus taking the action steps I needed for it to manifest into reality. There were times when I hit obstacles, but those provided wonderful opportunities to expand my mind in working out how I was going to get around, over, or through the obstacle. The biggest thing was that I never gave up, and neither should you.

Simply believe and be. YOU have that power within!

About Leyla Hur
Leyla Hur is an Empowerment and Inspirational Motivator, a speaker, author, host of the highly successful, internationally listened to, radio show, "Manifesting the Positive"; and Editor-in-Chief of "Magnify You" an online magazine dedicated to inspiring, informing, and transforming lives.

Learn more about Leyla's consultations and empowerment techniques by visiting http://LeylaHur.com and subscribe to her newsletter to receive your free e-book. Also, remember to visit http://MagnifyYou.com to magnify YOUR inner star.

Perseverance by Beth Wilson

I was just four months pregnant when I realized my marriage had to end. But after leaving a life in politics behind and beginning a doctoral program, I realized I'd have to hold on until my son was born to see what the next step was. Though the growing swell of my belly and my baby's frequent kicks gave me incredible joy, it was excruciating to think that there might not be a way to fix a damaging marriage, not even with a child on the way. I hoped that there might be a way to avoid the decision, when deep down I knew it had already been made. The bulk of my money was tied up in my education and persevering while still enjoying any magical moments seemed like a matter of survival.

On February 2nd the doctors lifted a beautifully formed eight-pound boy from my belly and, I had never experienced a deeper love than on that day. To me, Alexander was perfect with a head full of black hair, a delightfully rounded cherub face and searching blue-brown eyes. Once we arrived home from the hospital I discovered that Alexander had colic. He would cry inconsolably for long periods of time and no matter how hard I tried to soothe him my efforts were in vain. The pain and indigestion simply had to run their course so I struggled right along side him to provide any comfort I could. On top of that, he was a wakeful child, rarely napping and demanding to be fed five to ten times a night! His metabolism was faster than any our physician had ever seen and so I knew that to withhold feedings would be a mistake. I quickly came to understand why sleep deprivation is such an effective torture used throughout the world. But we soldiered on, and when necessary, got creative. Not wanting to lose one of their prize students, my professors allowed me to bring my son to class regardless of the fact that he slurped and burped and cooed. No one seemed to mind. In fact, more often than not, the other students were delighted to have him on the campus. But, after only a year, I had to drop out of university. I was simply too exhausted to manage all spheres of my life.

One day while I was resting in the sun as Alexander napped (a rare occurrence), a book idea popped into my head. Why not write a meditation-style book for new mothers and open up a new market while providing a great service? As soon as I'd made the decision to write the book, the page-a-day reflections started to pour out of me. All of the ups and downs, the joys and fears of motherhood spilled onto the page as though I was both observing this amazing transition at the same time as I was living it. Even when pinned to the couch by my voracious little eater, I jotted down my ideas as they spun through my thoughts. Never had I been more grateful for legal pads! Then, later in the evening when the house was quiet, since we were going to be up anyway, I'd nurse my son or simply rock him in my arms as I typed with my right hand, one finger, one letter at a time. In a matter of weeks I had enough material for a proposal that I quickly submitted to an agent. Waiting for his reply was exasperating. I was so impatient. Like a pregnant woman in her final trimester, I cleaned the house, and then cleaned it again, continuing to write daily pages for the book, confident it would sell.

When the agent finally got back to me, it was not only to tell me that he would represent me, but also that he had already sold the book to a wonderful publisher in New York City. I was ecstatic! Between play dates, forets to the park, swim class, highchair feedings, and changing diapers I worked tirelessly—and whenever my son fell asleep in the car on the way back from an excursion, I pulled over to the side of the road to write, yellow pad on the passenger seat.

As soon as my advance arrived, I tucked it away in savings, uncertain about my future—and it was a good thing I had. My marriage became worse and worse. The mind games, emotional terrorism and verbal violence were more than I could bear, yet I knew I couldn't leave just yet. There wasn't enough money to support a child and he was simply too young to leave in the care of others while I took a tradition job. I found it ironic that I had helped with the parental leave bill while working in Congress as a legislative assistant and yet ten years passed and I couldn't take advantage of it. Nevertheless, the time with my son was precious despite the difficulties swirling around us and I didn't want to miss a moment. I knew I could never get time with him back.

Then, tragedy struck. My stepbrother committed suicide, suddenly and without warning. I was shocked by the news and the loss. He had always been someone I enjoyed, loved and respected and the last time I saw him he seemed to be doing fine. Thankfully, the rigors of motherhood and my writings kept me grounded at a time when it wouldn't have been difficult to be consumed with grief and depression.

One day the phone rang and I tentatively answered it, hoping it wasn't more bad news. It wasn't. "Look at the front page of The Wall Street Journal," an excited voice on the other end of the receiver exclaimed, and there it was: my book had volume sales in its first five months out! My prayers had been answered and before I could bask in the glory of it all, I began a follow up book since my son was now entering the toddler years: *Meditations for Mothers of Toddlers.* Interestingly, my agent wouldn't sell it. (I found out later that he was stalling its release and "borrowing" some of my ideas to put in his own mediation book). Not being one to let others dictate my destiny, I went directly to the publisher and brokered my own book deal--and without the 15% commission, it felt all the sweeter.

Sadly, life with my husband was unworkable. When my first royalty check arrived, it was enough to support us for a year and so I moved out, with my son, to begin a new life. But the peace I was expecting was not forthcoming. The violence escalated and with it, I became ensnared in family court. In fact, I spent over sixteen years enmeshed in the insanity of our legal system—a system that is costly and highly ineffective. I still can hardly believe that I survived it; that we survived it. But we did...and all those years I wrote, I spoke, I tucked my son into bed, I took part-time jobs when needed and I met some amazing individuals who kept me going when I thought I had nothing left to give. I persisted and that has made all the difference. I loved and I was loved back. My legal costs exceeded 2.5 million dollars, yet I have created success. I have a wonderful child, now a bright and imaginative young man, with whom I have an incredible relationship. I have continued to forge new paths, transform other's lives, heal hearts and have healed my own heart. My latest book, *He's Just No Good For You: A Guide to Getting Out of a Destructive Relationship,* was published the same year my son turned eighteen and I was emancipated from the legal system. It is a testament to what I, and many other women, have endured—some of us for months, others for years. Aren't I fortunate to be able to make this contribution? Truly the joy of a writer...and now that *He's Just No Good For You* has been optioned for television, it's impact will continue to grow so that others, just like me, can live better lives and move beyond controlling and psychologically dominating men to find the love they truly deserve. The love we all deserve. I can't say it enough: persistence pays off.

About Beth Wilson

Beth Wilson is a best-selling author, speaker, Transformational Life Coach and mother. Her books include: *Meditations for New Mothers, Meditations for Mothers of Toddlers, Meditations During Pregnancy, Restoring Balance to a Mother's Busy Life, Creating Balance in Your Child's Life* and *He's Just No Good For You: A Guide to Leaving a Destructive Relationship.* Beth offers workshops for women's transformation and empowerment.

"The ultimate measure of a man is not where he stands in moments of comfort and convenience, but where he stands at times of challenge and controversy."
~Martin Luther King, Jr.

Choose to Live a Life of Joy by Karen Sherman, Ph.D.

Back in High School, I was the President of my Senior Class -- in fact, the first female ever to hold that position. To make it even more unusual, I ran against my boyfriend and won by four votes! He had suggested he run for President and that I run for Vice President. I couldn't do this, however, since it would have been a step down for me having already served as Jr. Class President. He had no interest in the 2nd position.

At the end of the year, the Seniors had an awards assembly, and my classmates had voted me "Most Stubborn." But as the Grade Advisor gave me the award, he said, I really should be called, "Most Persistent."

There were lots of other extracurricular activities that earned me that title; and it certainly sounds like I had an unusually successful run in high school -- something most teens do not experience. Was it all persistence? Perhaps, but in retrospect, I think it also had to do with getting out of my house. Luckily, I channeled that need into activities that were positive in nature. Since my home life was filled with constant dysfunction and tension, I couldn't stand being there. Doing various tasks at school was acceptable to my parents.

Escaping from what was upsetting by putting myself into school activities was a type of survival mode I employed for many years to come.

As an adult, I was married with two children all while running a thriving private practice as a psychologist. To the outside world, all looked right. But my internal life told a different story.

Having been the product of a significantly dysfunctional family, there were lots of leftover wounds. I doubted my self-worth and always felt like something was missing. I had been the victim of every type of abuse there was. In my opinion, neglect was the worst. As a result, my behavior was either an attempt to gain the approval and love from my parents or to hide from my pain in self-defeating actions.

Throughout my life, I craved my mother's attention and time. Since my father was so awful to me, I wished for his demise. It seemed as though he was the one who stood in the way of having a relationship with her. (I know how terrible that sounds but he really was quite toxic to me.) Then, one day, it happened -- he passed away! Initially, my mom and I had the relationship I had dreamed about for years, though most of it was by phone since we lived in different states.

I anxiously set up a visit with her. Much to my overwhelming disappointment, upon spending an intense and concentrated amount of time with her, I realized that she really was not emotionally present; in fact, upon serious reflection, she never was. In reality, it was not my father who had stood in the way; it was her inability to be emotionally available that kept us apart. My childhood dream was crushed; the fantasy that I had held onto for all my life was not to be.

This realization threw me into a terrible tailspin; I emotionally hit bottom. To this day, I don't know how I managed to do the things I needed to. Still functioning as a Psychologists in private practice, more than once, I would be in my bed and come out to see a client, only to return to bed once the session was over. At times, the pain was so great, I didn't know if I could bear it.

But, my persistence surfaced. I was not going to let my past define me and take away the possibilities of the wonderful life I now had. I chose to face my pain and to heal my old wounds. Yes, it was work. But as a result of this experience, not only can I say that I am free of my old ghosts, I am a better wife, mother, and therapist.

I came to realize that a different type of intervention was needed to help people get past their past. As a result, I decided that it was important to share the tools I used to help myself and wrote an award-winning self-help book, "Mindfulness and The Art of Choice: Transform Your Life."

Even getting the book published and known has been a commitment and taken steadfastness. But then steadfastness is a synonym for persistence!

I earned that award so many years ago -- I guess my Grade Advisor knew what he was saying and I can truly say that I know that persistence can pay off!

About Dr. Karen Sherman

Dr. Karen Sherman, a NY licensed psychologist, has been practicing over 20 years focusing on relationships/marriage and helping people achieve their greatest potential. Karen authored "Mindfulness and The Art of Choice: Transform Your Life" enabling people to let go of conditioned responses and empowering them to make their own choices, co-authored "Marriage Magic! Find It, Keep It, and Make It Last," and contributed to "101 Great Ways to Improve Your Life, Vol. 2," writing about overcoming stress. She's a featured writer on Yahoo Personals, a relationship blogger for ThirdAge.com, and writes for Hitchedmag.com. To Find Out More visit www.drkarensherman.com.

Good Enough Is Not Enough by Masha Malka

I often think that it is more difficult to succeed in life for kids who are talented and gifted than for those who are not because when things don't come so easy to you, you learn to work hard and be persistent to initially achieve the same results that come easy to others...

Yet, as time goes by and children grow into adults, it is those who are not afraid of hard work and who are determined to complete tasks no matter how hard or even impossible it might seem in the beginning become the real winners in life and achieve extraordinary results!

Fortunately, I was one of those kids who had to work hard to get results in most areas of my life which gave me the strength do deal with a difficult time in my life when I became a Soviet refugee at the age of 17 to the United States of America.

Leaving my friends, most of my family and my citizenship, behind with all of the material possessions, except a small suitcase and less than $ 100 per person, my parents, little brother, sick grandfather, and I arrived to a completely foreign country to start a new life. With no language, contacts, and knowledge of the American culture it was an overwhelming task.

I remember thinking to myself, "What can a little Russian girl in a big, powerful, fascinating, and, at the time, scary country as the USA, do to make a difference?" I didn't even speak their language! And, I had no idea what I wanted to do – I had no real purpose in life and felt lost and confused.

Yet, just 2 decades later I am living an extraordinary life – the life that was once only a dream, the life where I am happily married with 3 children, where work and play feel like the same thing, where I have the freedom to do what I want and when I want it. I live in a very beautiful place, have lots of real friends, and most importantly, a life where I like who I am, feel that I am making a difference and am excited about the future!

How did I make such a huge shift from a lost and insecure refugee to a powerful woman who loves her life? By making a commitment to myself that I will never settle for second best!

This meant that I stopped finding excuses for abusive relationships, uninteresting and underpaid jobs, and a life without meaning and purpose. It also meant that I stopped living a life that pleased others and not me – from that moment on I decided to live my life on my own terms, make my own mistakes and not regret anything.

My life began to change rapidly and so did my circle of friends. At first I felt lonely in my new-found freedom but then I started meeting new like-minded people, moved to Europe, got married, gave birth to my first baby and went back to school to get a graduate degree. I still had plenty of doubts and fears but it was a good start and I knew that if I just keep taking little steps in the right direction I will get there eventually.

I never liked being average. Good enough is not enough for me. I am not a perfectionist but I do have high standards for myself and some self-imposed rules that I've been following.

Here are some of my rules:

1. Finish what I start
2. Don't get involved in something I do not enjoy doing
3. Be proud of my work before I let anyone else see it
4. Put my ego aside, and request constructive feedback in order to improve
5. Learn something new every day
6. Be kind to myself – speak kindly to myself; acknowledge and celebrate my small and big successes; take time to get pampered and do the things that fulfill me
7. Listen to my heart - make final decisions based on my intuition rather than logic
8. Be grateful for all that I have and don't have and for all that I have become and still striving to become
9. Be clear about my purpose and goals and persist until I get there. My definition of failure is not making mistakes or falling down, but in giving up and staying down.
10. Anything is possible if I am willing to invest my time and effort and be patient.

The freedom to be who you are is the greatest freedom of all and I am fortunate to have found this freedom, which for me is my greatest achievement so far.

In my best-selling book, *The One Minute Coach: change your life one minute at a time*, I emphasize that to create change and to live your best life you don't need to be a genius, well-connected, highly educated, young, old, or anything else except someone who *really* wants it and is willing to do what it takes to get it.

You have what it takes to be extraordinary so don't settle for anything less that that!

About Masha Malka
Masha Malka is a mother of 3, an international speaker, success coach, best-selling author of The One Minute Coach: change your life one minute at a time book, Discover Your Inborn Genius e-book, contributing author to the Chicken Soup for the Soul: Power Moms book and a resident coach for Talk Radio Europe.
Masha dedicates her life to helping people create balance and positivity on the way to their dream lives. She also encourages and helps people to unleash their potential and achieve their greatness. Please visit www.mashamalka.com to find out more.

"If your ship doesn't come in, swim out to meet it."
~Johathan Winters

The Power of Persistent Belief, Vision, and Actions By Dr. Joe Rubino

Over the course of the past 18 years ever since I reinvented my life from an introverted and resigned dentist to an empowered life optimization coach, motivational speaker, and personal development author, I have found that the qualities of persistency and consistency, when combined with a powerful and compelling vision AND high self esteem, can result in some truly incredible manifestations. Before I share my own story of persistency with you, allow me to explain how these components combine to produce magic.

First and foremost, all accomplishment and manifestation is preceded by thought. We are either reactively at the affect of our own negative self-talk and the thoughts of others, or we are taking responsibility for creating a series of thoughts that make up a powerful vision to inspire and propel our lives forward with velocity. An inspirational and moving vision necessarily encompasses all six key aspects of our lives, namely our health and appearance, our wealth and finances, our business or occupation, our family and other relationships, the area of our personal and spiritual development, and what we do to recreate, have fun, and pursue our passions. It also must certainly involve others, not just ourselves in order to be complete and inspiring.

I recommend creating a vivid, emotionally-rich written vision that describes a brief movie clip at some future point in time that fully provides a clear and exciting view of who we will be, what we will do at work and at play, what we will have surrounding us in our world, and what people and causes we will contribute to...to have our vision be richly rewarding and inspire us to action. When we read such a compelling vision daily and can picture its manifestation as inevitable, we will generate the required self-motivation needed to bring it about on purpose. Our minds can not chemically distinguish reality from such a clear and moving vision so that if we bathe ourselves in the emotions, sights, sounds, and feelings that such a vivid vision provides and we see its realization as all but guaranteed, we will be empowered to make it so through our actions.

This is where high self esteem and belief in our inevitable success comes in. Without it, we will find a way to sabotage our efforts, invalidate our abilities, ignore the serendipitous opportunities that would otherwise become obvious, and generate a self-fulfilling prophesy that says "I knew I couldn't accomplish that *because*..." We then get to be right about our lacking faith in ourselves and the eventual accomplishment of our dreams and feel sorry for ourselves while attracting the pity of others! To the contrary, those possessing high self-esteem see any obstacles in their path as temporary challenges or opportunities for discovery that will ultimately lead to success and accomplishment. As a result, armed with this certainty about one's eventual outcome being successful, those possessing a powerful vision and unwavering belief in themselves will be in action consistently (day in and day out or at least on a regular basis) and persistently (following up with a positive expectation of success for as long as is necessary.)

Before I share my story of persistence with you, I wish to paint a picture of what my life looked like before discovering the awesome power of positive expectation, vision, and persistent, committed action. In 1990, I was a practicing dentist with two successful practices by society's standards. Our practices attracted about 250 new patients each month, we had the appreciation and respect of our patients and colleagues and we made a lot of money. But for me, something important was certainly missing. I felt trapped by my practice and feared that dentistry was the only thing I could do to earn a living for my family. Through a rigorous personal development program, I discovered that I need not continue to live with the resigned sadness of doing something that I was no longer passionate about. I discovered that my core values of contribution, inspiration, creativity, and fun were not being honored and I learned that I could not only honor my values by reinventing myself, but I could successfully champion others to do the same and lead their best lives! As I discovered my gifts and declared my new life purpose to be a champion of others to lead their best lives marked by high self-esteem and positive expectation, my entire world opened up. I began to see and act upon opportunity after opportunity that would take me to the life I love today as a writer, life and business coach, and creator of structures, tools and systems that allow people to be their best and live their best lives. By acting on my vision persistently, day after day, I discover new chances to move my new life and career forward as I likewise champion people to step into their own magnificence and move their lives and businesses forward with passion and velocity.

An amazing thing happened when I declared that my vision would be to impact the lives of 20 million people by the year 2015. (Remember, I was the guy others joked could not lead three people in silent prayer!) People and opportunities consistent with this declared vision began to show up everywhere for me. My commitment was to take some focused action on a daily basis that would move my vision in a forward direction. It did not matter that I had no idea how I could cause this vision to manifest. My job was not to micromanage how it all would unfold; it was simply to act persistently in alignment with this vision and be open to guidance from God, my guides and the Universe, knowing that I would be able to attract the right people, resources, and opportunities to bring it about.

The latest development in alignment with my vision has been a partnership with an accomplished West Coast movie studio that has committed to develop my three personal development fables into a movie trilogy that will touch the lives of millions in way that I could not envision when the whole process of reinventing myself began. I am now clear that our job is not to wait until the circumstances are just right before we act. It is to gain clarity on what is important to us, enjoy the process and learn from every challenge and opportunity, clarify and tweak our visions as we go, and take persistent and consistent action in the direction of our dreams.

As Gothe once said, "Whatever you think you can do or believe you can do, begin it. Action has magic, grace, and power in it."

About Dr. Joe Rubino

Dr. Joe Rubino is an internationally acclaimed expert on the topic of self-esteem, a life-changing personal development trainer and success coach and best selling author of 9 books and 2 Audio sets on topics ranging from how to restore self-esteem, achieve business success, maximize joy and fulfillment in life and productivity in business. An acclaimed speaker and course leader, he is known for his groundbreaking work in personal and leadership development, building effective teams, enhancing listening and communication skills, life and business coaching and optimal life planning.

The Kindness Cure by CJ Scarlet

When my doctor told me in 2002 that my debilitating autoimmune conditions (Lupus and Scleroderma) had caused me to develop a progressive heart condition, life came to a screeching halt. My life was already marred by a series of traumatic events and tragic mistakes, and my death sentence felt like an apt ending to an unfulfilled life. Desperately ill and debilitated, I struggled to make the best of my remaining time, but my overwhelming fear and misery overrode my attempts to be happy and robbed me of hope.

One day about a year-and-a-half later, I was given the opportunity to meet with a Tibetan lama. I poured out my tale of woe, fully expecting the Lama to pour sympathy upon my deserving head. But that's not what happened. Instead, the Lama ordered me with fierce compassion to stop feeling sorry for myself and focus my attention on the happiness of others. Although I had been a victims' advocate for years, I had been so focused on my own suffering, that I had become oblivious to the needs of others.

Out of obedience, curiosity, and more than a bit of boredom, I began helping others, saying prayers when an ambulance would pass and letting the mom with the screaming baby go ahead of me in line at the grocery store. I noticed that when I did something to benefit another, I felt a flush of happiness. What I didn't know was that at the physiological level, each act of kindness caused my body to released pain-killing endorphins and depression-fighting serotonin, which offered a boost to my immune system and decreased the stress chemicals that were so deadly to my body. I began to do more, giving my cane to a woman who was struggling to walk and volunteering at the Red Cross after Hurricane Katrina.

The real turn-around occurred when I realized, I mean really *got*, that I alone am responsible for my own happiness. This insight was prompted by a random act of kindness I did out of desperation. On this particular day, I was feeling really negative and angry because I felt like my family wasn't appreciating me. My pity party was quickly evolving into a grand pity ball when I realized that I felt really awful being consumed by such negative thoughts. I thought about what would make me feel better and decided it would be offering a gift to someone else. So I picked up the phone and dialed a random local number, getting the voicemail of some computer technician. I left the following message: "You don't know me, but I want to tell you that even if the people in your life forget to tell you, YOU are appreciated!" I hung up the phone with a huge smile on my face and genuine gratitude in my heart. In just *ten seconds* I went from feeling bitter and miserable to feeling fantastic, and it was all because I performed an act of kindness.

My next big opportunity came one night while I was eating alone at a restaurant. At the table behind me were two women talking about how hard things had become since one of the women's husband had lost his job. The wife said she was working three jobs, but still didn't have any money to buy gas to get to work the next day. She said she prayed all the time for help. The friend sympathized and then they got up and left, parting in the parking lot. I approached the woman and told her I couldn't help overhearing her words, and asked if she would allow me to give her money to buy gas. The women looked shocked and stammered that she couldn't possibly accept money from a stranger. I looked at her steadily and asked her if she really prayed for a solution. She said yes. Then I said, "What if this is the answer to your prayer." Well, she started crying and I started crying, and she agreed to let me buy her a tank of gas. I truly felt like the universe was working through me to answer the prayer of this woman.

> "No one can make you feel inferior without your consent."
> ~ Eleanor Roosevelt

The more kindness I extended, the happier I became. I reached a state of such joy that it no longer mattered whether I lived or died; I was happy either way. And the happier I became, the better I felt, until, just two years later, my physical problems—all of them—began reversing themselves.

This time when I presented myself to the Lama, he was amazed by my progress and commanded me to write books and give speeches about what I had learned that had so dramatically changed my life. Within a 24-hour period, I wrote the basis of *Neptune's Gift*, the idea based on a short allegorical tale told by Mitch Albom in *Tuesdays with Morrie*. Writing *Neptune's Gift*, which mega-author Jack Canfield calls "the next *Jonathan Livingston Seagull*, and re-igniting my career as an advocate and motivational speaker has brought even greater joy to my life. Today my health is better than it was when I first became ill 19 years ago. I am now devoted to spending the remaining years of my life to helping others achieve the happiness they crave and deserve.

On World Kindness Day in November 2008, I launched the Kindness Cure Campaign (www.thekindnesscure.org)—a movement designed to motivate people to help me perform one million acts of kindness in one year. To accomplish this, I created a social networking site and am performing 365 acts of kindness myself, many of which are being digitally recorded to show people how very simple it is to be kind to others. So my advice to others is simple, to get what you want, give it away to another. That is the real secret of happiness.

About CJ Scarlet
CJ Scarlet is an award-winning author, motivational speaker and certified "Courage Coach." She has given speeches and workshops at state, national, and international events. She was recently featured in the national bestseller, *Happy for No Reason*, by Marci Shimoff, in which she was named one of the "Happy 100" people on the planet.

"Do not go where the path may lead, go instead where there is no path and leave a trail."
~ Ralph Waldo Emerson

Work on Your Waistline by Derrick Hayes

I walked in the building to clock in for work one day and I overheard two women talking about me. I don't think I was supposed to hear their conversation. The first lady said, "He's cute, but just a little bigger then I like them". The other lady said, "You are right, He has the dunlap disease, where his belly dunlap over his waist."

My two co-workers were telling truth even though it hurt. Late that night I took my shirt off and looked in the mirror at my self and said, "there has to be a better way".

I called Larry Paul who is a certified strength and conditioning specialist and owner of *FACES Fitness and Conditioning, Inc.* to ask for his advice on how to lose weight. The advice Larry gave me I was really not ready for. Mr. Paul recommended that that I either get a colon cleanse or start eating a high fiber diet. According to his research over the years, there are people that are walking around with an extra 10 to 20 pounds of waste in their colon.

I knew I needed to eat healthier and exercise more in order to look and feel better. I had to do my own research and I realized that over the last 30 years my diet was not that good and there definitely was concern for me to make the necessary changes.

I decided not to go with the colon cleanse. I found some information on fiber. I used to hear a saying, "An apple a day will keep the Dr. away." I always knew what it said but I did not recognize the importance of the apple. Apples and other Fruits and vegetable width='100%' contain fiber in them that can help remove toxins and waste from your body. Fiber is here to help remove the waste to keep you from being sick and also help prevent future illnesses.

When I research how to live better, I receive quality information on how to improve my life. I was on a break in between work and watching the Oprah Winfrey Show where she had Dr. Oz on. The segment was on how to read food labels. After watching the show I knew I needed to stay away from foods with labels that read high fructose corn syrup, partially hydrogenated, or sugar.

After the show I went grocery shopping. I wanted to get some cereal because it was food that I could easily eat in one setting and get my day off to a good start. As I started to read the labels on the boxes of cereal I realized that there is a lot of cereal that is not healthy for us. I based this on what I learned from The Oprah Winfrey Show.

After about 30 minutes in the cereal isle I found what I was looking for. I found was Fiber One, a cereal that had no sugar and 14g of fiber with every half cup. I knew that since we need 25 to 30 grams of fiber a day that this would definitely get me off to a good start. I started to take my life higher by eating a bowl of Fiber One for breakfast each morning.

Even in the beginning when I would tell other people what I was doing they would have two responses. One response was that eating fiber would give you diarrhea or that they just couldn't stand the taste.

The truth is that when you increase fiber in your diet you will likely have more bowel movements. Most people I talk to have only one bowel movement a day. This change in your diet should not cause you to have diarrhea.

The taste was the other thing I had to deal with. You can add flavor to the cereal by adding raisins, bananas, and apples from time to time. When I run out of milk I add the cereal into oatmeal. You can eat it in your salad as croutons or top off your yogurt with a healthy crunch.

Along with exercise fiber is not the only thing you should eat. Please consult with your physician so that they can properly plan a breakthrough system for you. I'm writing this article because I know there is someone else out there just like me. The results I have seen in a little over three months have been incredible. I lost 25 pounds and two inches in my waist.

Once I began to eat better and exercise more it gave me more energy to get me through the day. I have been able to accomplish more while sleeping less. I started with the fiber then I was able to keep changing other things about my diet. One thing leads to another and I even brought my cholesterol down 30 plus points.

Find a twenty-pound weight and put it in your book bag and carry it around all day. This is the extra weight that I had been carrying around the last ten years. Then when you remove the bag you will know what it will be like once you make the necessary changes in your life. If you are one who does not need to lose weight please research your diet because your colon can still be full of waste, toxins, and eventually diseases that can lead to death.

I'm usually a happy person but now I'm ecstatic. When I look in the mirror I see what you can see. I went from 235 down to 205. It has been over eight years since I could even think about being close to 200 pounds.

What do you have to lose? Only a few pounds and some negative lifestyle habits. I had to change my thinking just like you do. We all can be transformed by the renewing of our minds (Romans 12:2). If this information does not apply to you in this article then do the next best thing and pass this on to a friend or loved one.

I hear things like this all the time. "I have wasted my life away." "They are just a waste of time." My waste used to be my waist. Men, you can lose 15 to 20 pounds and get into a new pair of stylish pants. Women, you can now be empowered to wear the dress of your dreams.

I came back to work after coming off vacation and now people were recognizing my new look. The two women I had mentioned earlier wanted to know what I was doing to take my life to another level. The same advice I gave them is the same advice that I will leave you with. If you want to look fine then "Work On Your Waste Line."

About Derrick Hayes
Derrick Hayes, an alumnus of Tennessee State University is available for small and large meetings, church events, academic speaking engagements and workshops. Please visit Derrick's website at http://www.DerrickHayes.com and to book him for a speaking engagement or media event, send an email to info@DerrickHayes.com.

Persisting from Q, W, E, R, T by Shirley Cheng

"Q, W, E, R, T," I mumbled, hitting each key with my left index finger. I finished going through that row before moving to the row beneath it. I kept my fingers from exploring the keys other than the main letters and numbers so I would not set off something I would be unable to fix. Was I a student learning to type on a computer for the first time? Not quite. My first time typing on a computer was in sixth grade, and the following year, I was surprised with my very own personal computer when I arrived home from school, and that was five years ago. So why was I going through the keys like someone who was touching the keyboard for the first time?

Z, X, C, V, B, N, M. I smiled when I had gone through all the rows of the letter keys for the first time as a blind individual. The general position of the keys was not foreign to me, but the keyboard was. My school district was lending me this laptop, equipped with all the neat software I had never heard of before. There was the Dragon Naturally Speaking program that could catch the words I spoke into a microphone and type them for me, as well as the screen reader JAWS that would read back what was typed, and I seldom liked what I heard, so here I was, resolving to type correct words rather than having Mr. Dragon make a zillion mistakes for me to fix, which resulted in even more mistakes. Yes, I was determined to type. Maybe I would not achieve eighty words per minute with just two index fingers, one of which could not even bend and both of which were touched with severe juvenile rheumatoid arthritis, I would be satisfied with typing forty words. Well, okay, thirty words per minute sounded nice to my ears right now.

After my fingers had explored all the letters and

> "I thank God for my handicaps, for through them, I have found myself, my work and my God."
> ~Helen Keller

numbers, I ventured to type my first word. Using my left index finger, I felt my way to the letter S and tapped it. Next, I moved to the right until I got to H and hit it. It was the letter I's turn. I hovered my finger above the right area of the keyboard and pressed down a key. JAWS announced, "O." Alright, I did not expect to get all the letters correct the first time, as I had no fixed position with my hands. But I was determined to get it down to the letter, no pun intended. I fingered my way to the Backspace, promising myself that it would not be a key I would frequently use. I expected to type like a good-enough pro soon, picturing my fingers flying over the keyboard. Boy, was I thrilled when that "soon" was much sooner than I expected, and that pro was definitely more than "good enough.

As days passed, I became more and more familiar with the laptop as I practiced typing, and in a few weeks, that familiarity allowed me to type with relative ease. With ease came speed. My ability to type one complete word steadily turned into a fulfillment of my initial goal: typing thirty words per minute. Yet, that initial goal was easily surpassed soon afterward.

"You were even worried that you couldn't keep up with me on the IM, but you're one of the fastest people I know," JAWS read my best friend's observation when we chatted online via the instant messenger.

I grinned broadly. Just two months ago, I was hungering to simply touch the keyboard; now, not only could I type e-mails, short stories, and poems, but I also could surf the Internet and keep in touch with my friends via the IM. Do you know what else? I could even type faster than before I had my eyesight! I had definitely achieved a gold medal.

"It's so wonderful that you can use a computer now!" gushed my mother, breaking into my thoughts. She sat down next to me, taking a look at my computer screen.

I pushed my hands against the table edge, sending my wheelchair back a notch. I leaned back with contentment. "Yes, I can't believe it. I had not thought that I could actually use a computer like a sighted person.

I can do almost everything using JAWS." A surge of gratitude swept over me for the inventor of this piece of software that must have changed the lives of so many visually impaired people, and I know it was ready to change mine next.

"And you figured out everything all by yourself! No one is here to teach you anything." Mom was right. Although the school sent a lady who set up the assistive technology for me and introduced the basics to get me started, I was alone to do the rest. I had to figure out how to navigate all the programs without using a mouse, discover all the secret shortcuts implemented by specific key combinations, and find out the best way in utilizing JAWS to maximize my computer experience.

"I love figuring out things. It's easy."

"Easy for you. I can't even begin to imagine how you do it."

I shrugged. Ever since I was a little girl, I always enjoyed figuring out how to use something, be it a new VCR set or a mathematical problem.

Every challenge brought me excitement.

"You're always so persistent."

I laughed. "Right on!" Whenever I began a new task, I would have already envisioned my achievement in the end, motivating me forward and strengthening my determination. Thus, this was the case with my newfound adventure.

What was next in store for me? What else could I do with my renewed virtual delight? Would I be able to make websites like the eighty-six I created when I was sixteen, a year prior to my eyesight loss? I found out less than a year later, and what lay ahead was nothing I had ever expected before (it seemed I did not expect a lot of things, eh?).

***

I ran my index finger down the length of the spine, enjoying its cool sensation. I flipped through the book, at first taking each page between my fingers to feel its crispness. In my mind's eye, I pictured the words against the off-white paper.

My own spine tingled with something indescribable as I felt the newly printed book in my hands. How thrilled was I to hold a book; but it was not just any book--it was my book.

I sighed blissfully. I thought back to my first time using a computer without eyesight, the first words I had typed, not knowing that those first words would lead me to a new career as an author. It all seemed like a dream, but I knew it was as real and solid as my book in my hands.

I had certainly gone a long way; from urging myself to

type, to writing my first book, to formatting my subsequent manuscripts, to completing every self-publishing task on my own, to designing and maintaining my website, and to typing at the speed of about seventy words per minute.

And now, at age twenty-six, nearly seven years since the day I pressed Q, W, E, R, T, I have become an award-winning author with twenty book awards, able to touch others by bringing humor, hope, and healing into their lives.

What is my ultimate secret to success? The power of persistence? Indeed, I would not have been able to achieve what I have accomplished without this power, but it is not my ultimate secret. That secret lies in the fact that this power is gifted to me by my spirituality. It has been bestowing upon me this power since my birth, from the persistence to overcoming my multiple physical disabilities and blindness to the persistence to achieving grade level after only about 180 days of school attendance in my lifetime, and now the persistence to making a positive difference not only in my life but in others as well. With this power, it is up to me to persistently build on it to accomplish what I am destined to achieve. Again I wonder, what is in store for me next? I can hardly wait to find out.

About the Shirley Cheng:
Shirley Cheng (b. 1983), a blind and physically disabled award-winning author (with twenty book awards, including Mom's Choice Awards and nine Parent to Parent Adding Wisdom Awards), motivational speaker, self-empowerment expert, poet, author of nine books, contributor to seventeen, and a parental rights advocate, has had severe juvenile rheumatoid arthritis since infancy. Owing to years of hospitalization, she received no education until age eleven. Back then, she knew only her ABCs and very simple English;

other than that, her book knowledge was non-existent. However, after only about 180 days of special education in elementary school, she mastered grade level in all areas and entered a regular sixth grade class in middle school. Unfortunately, Shirley lost her eyesight at the age of seventeen. After a successful eye surgery, she hopes to earn multiple science doctorates from Harvard University.
Visit www.ShirleyCheng.com for more inspiration.

"A journey of one thousand miles begins with a single step." ~ Confucius

From Kid to Author: A Story of Sticking to Goals By Kimberly Carolan

Growing up, I always felt like it was easy to quit. My parents made it easy believing that they were being compassionate when "the going got tough". If anything was "too hard", I was allowed to quit. The list started getting long with activities that I could "quit" mid-season: T-ball, gymnastics, cheerleading, flute, etc. I don't think they could stomach me crying after getting hit in the head with a baseball or not being able to do a cartwheel well in gymnastics. But quitting did not help me either. Truth be told, there were things that I continued throughout their duration, too: Dance, swimming, diving, piano lessons and marching band, among other activities. But I had wished that even if I had not "gone pro" with baseball or gymnastics that I would have at least finished my season with the group. I felt like a looser when my friends continued the season while I opted out of the pain of practice, getting hurt or embarrassment from not being born with talent in a given area.

When I got near college age, I realized that this type to behavior would not get me anywhere. If I quit in the middle of college, for example, I would never get a degree and I would limit my career potential. So, even though it was hard, I finished school and got a B.S. in Business. But the quitting started again with crazy bosses and work environments, so I eventually became an entrepreneur. Eventually, though, times got tough as an entrepreneur. My first career move into entrepreneurship started as a real estate agent. While I was excited while starting out and had some promising business, my enthusiastic demeanor eventually quailed. Concurrently, the market was fledgling in my area, too, so real estate was not really a viable option anymore.

I took a long, hard look at life. What was I really interested in? What was I passionate about? What really mattered? Life is short, and I had to make whatever I did matter and I needed to finish what I started. So I moved cross-country to a new place with new people and new opportunities and I started writing about whatever I could think of. Then I started getting more specific and started writing solely about grief. You see, while I was still in college, my dad died unexpectedly of cancer. And I saw a huge opportunity to reach out to hurting people and to educate people about what people are up against when a loved one dies. This was my new vision in life: To help encourage grievers and to give friends surrounding the bereaved ways to encourage their grieving friends.

I forced myself to finish against the odds: Against critics, against angry relatives, against my own doubts and against my own innate lack of discipline. I had a plan to do enough research and write a certain amount of pages per day until I was done. It did not matter if the pages were completely perfect or if they even made it to the final edition—I just had to keep writing. Now my book, *Walking through the Valley of the Shadow of Death* (Copyright © 2009, AEG Publishing) is out, I am working still on promotions and I will not stop until everything is finished.

I am glad now that I am learning to be more disciplined and finish what I have started. No matter how big a project is, it can get done. It just takes time, a plan and a positive attitude. Even hard things can be learned; impossible things can be done—it just takes commitment and not giving up.

And truly, the hardest obstacles to overcome were all obstacles within me. My lack of discipline absolutely needed to change. That was simple, in some ways: I needed a plan and simply needed to stick to it. A professor in college said this: "We always say that we don't have the time, but really the truth is that we choose to not make the time." These words rang in my ears as I began the project. I needed to choose to make the time, period.

But, of the forces within myself, my own self-doubts were the most paralyzing of all. I had lots of negative thoughts in my own head about how my book would never work out, that it would never be received or not be liked. A lot of times, just saying those things aloud to my husband who would encourage me really helped. It made those crazy ideas seem less "big" in my head. So anytime a person is undergoing a big project, you need a cheerleader to believe in you, like I did.

It was also quite difficult to deal with negative people while writing my book. There were lots of people that wanted to throw in their ideas and opinions about what I would write, if writing a book was worthwhile, and if writing what I was writing about was worthwhile. I simply avoided the intensely negative people. But there were negative people in my sphere that I could not avoid. The ones that I could not avoid, I simply did not talk about my book with them. If they asked about my book by chance, I would give positive and intentionally vague details. The fewer details, the less they had to call into question. I did not need to be discouraged by these people from the "peanut gallery". I figured that they could write whatever they wanted to in their own book and not superimpose their content into my book. I needed to be around positive people who could help me, not hinder me. My project was difficult enough without being swayed by naysayers.

And now I am continuing along the same road: Continuing promoting my book no matter what. I have a worthwhile vision that has, in the core, a desire to help people. But most of my difficulties have come from me. The ones outside of me have been deal with more and more by surrounding myself with positive people and avoid negative people.

About Kimberly Carolan
Kimberly Carolan is the President of Carolan Creative Enterprises, LLC. Author of Walking through the Valley of the Shadow of Death. Pianist and vocals for Clear Gray Sky, Seattle's newest jazz band. To learn more about Kimberly visit http://walkingthroughthevalleyoftheshadow.blogspot.com/

The Art of Financial Persistence by Stephanie J Hale

Imagine this, your mom comes to visit and there's a hooker making out with a client in broad daylight right by your garden gate. Or this, you're collecting your 5-year-old from school and have to walk past a drug dealer standing in a cloud of cannabis smoke. As you pass, he mutters, "wanna buy?" under his breath. Your son thinks the powder he's selling is candy. Or even this, a friend drops by and there's a wino sleeping in a pool of urine right by your front door. Every night, you hear men fighting outside, women screaming, and cars getting smashed.

That was my life 9 years ago. Let me tell you, it wasn't a lot of fun. My car was written off by joy riders within weeks of us moving in. My handbag was nicked by one of my neighbors while I was unloading my groceries. He went straight to the supermarket and spent over £200 before I even had time to call my credit card company. I couldn't hang out washing without it getting stolen. I lost count of the times I had to call the police because of attempted break-ins to my home.

The question is: how did I get here? One minute I'd been living in a nice house, driving a nice car, leading a nice lifestyle in a nice part of the city. The next, WHOOMPH! Pretty much overnight, I was divorced, broke, and wondering what hit me. Ok, there are worse places on earth and I had enough money to buy food. But it certainly wasn't somewhere you'd want to bring up kids.

It was one of the worst things that ever happened to me. But strangely enough, it was also one of the best. Up to this point, I'd taken little responsibility for my financial destiny. Savings & investments? B-o-r-i-n-g!

Financial spreadsheets. You what? Monthly outgoings? Ask my husband.

I knew how to work in a job and 'get by'. In fact, I had a string of professional positions many people would envy. Not particularly well-paid jobs – but jobs that sound great on paper, if you know what I mean. I'd worked for 15 years as a broadcaster and newsreader, and later as an Oxford University lecturer. People used to fly in from all over the world to attend my classes. "What a perfect job you have," they'd say. Oh yes, my job sounded great. But I'll tell you what: the people who envied me didn't see my pay slips or know I was working 70-hour weeks! I loved my work, but it certainly didn't pay enough money for anything but the basics.

Truth was, I didn't have the first clue on how to manage money, how to invest money, how to grow money. It just wasn't something that was on my agenda. I had been walking into disaster with my eyes wide shut - like so many people who blindly hope for the best. If I hadn't found this out when my marriage broke up, I sure as hell would have found out when I hit retirement age!

So what happened next? I spent the next five years reading everything I could get my hands on. I'll never forget the first book I read – 'Rich Dad Poor Dad' by Robert Kyosaki. That was a big awakening for me, a real shake-up of everything I'd ever believed or taken for granted. It struck a particular chord with me as it compared the fate of an 'educated Dad' who died broke, with that of an uneducated Dad who was financially free. I knew I was going to end up like the educated Dad too, unless I took radical action. From then on, I read books by Robert Allen, Jack Canfield, Mark Victor Hansen, Napoleon Hill, etc. I attended webinars, went to seminars, signed up to just about every newsletter going, and sought out mentors. I was working full-time, as well as evenings and weekends, to make ends meet. But in my free time, all I did was study.

Initially, I learned to trade equities, forex, and commodities. Then, as I developed a talent for trading, I was able to become a traders' coach with one of the UK's top trading schools. I set up my own business focusing on my big passion - publishing. I started giving my own talks and holding seminars. This year, I've launched the annual Women Millionaires' Bootcamp in the UK, together with a JV partner, to help other people learn how to grow their wealth and boost their businesses.

Hurdles? Yes, there have been plenty of them along the way. Friends have let me down. People have turned out to be untrustworthy. I've made stupid mistakes that have lost me money. I've launched projects that have flopped dramatically or failed to make a dime.

> "Great works are preformed not by strength but by perseverance."
> ~Samuel Johnson

There have been days when I've just felt like giving up. And always, there's been a nagging guilt that I haven't been a good Mom because I've had to spend so much time working.
High points? For every low point, there has definitely been a high point. There's been the kindness of numerous millionaires who have taken me under their wing - a half-hour here, lunch there, lengthy phone calls. There have been powerful tips and secrets that have boosted my business. Then, there's been the sharing with other traders and entrepreneurs on the same journey. Every day, I've felt myself growing in knowledge. Slowly, but surely, I've come to understand the principles that all seemed so incomprehensible when I first heard them. Until they have become a part of me – as natural as breathing. Most

importantly, there's the knowledge that when my kids look at me, they see freedom and choice – rather than a distraught mother who's worried about making ends meet. They can choose this same path if they want to. They can see that they have a choice.

I wish I could tell you that the journey has been easy. But initially, at least, there was a lot of hard work and a sharp learning curve. Did I ever feel like giving up? Absolutely. Was it terrifying? Sure – especially in the early days. Has it been worth it? Would I recommend it to anyone else? My God, yes!!!!

These days, with the divorce rate at 1 in 3, no one can afford to sleepwalk like I was. Even in the strongest marriage, women outlive men by 10 years. So if any of this rings bells with you, then it's time to start taking action. The pain of those years gave me the electric jolt I needed to turn my life around. If I can save just one person or child from experiencing the same pain I went through, I'll be happy.

If you haven't already done so, start educating yourself about wealth today. Read just one book. Next week, read another book. The week after that, read another. Never stop educating yourself. Just keep putting one foot in front of the other. Eventually, you'll reach the top of the mountain. With faith and courage, you can achieve anything.

About Stephanie J. Hale
Stephanie J Hale is an author, speaker and millionaire mindset expert. She is also CEO of the annual Women Millionaires Bootcamp in the UK. FREE newsletter at www.WomenMillionairesBootcamp.com.

Making Progress, Page By Page - By Kyle and Brady Baldwin

We grew up with a quote in our house that said, "There are no big moments you can reach only a series of small moments which you can stand upon." This quote from the play Autumn Garden has been inspirational to us as we set up My Own Book, a non-profit organization to spread the joy of reading. We started the program as a way to show younger kids that reading is fun and we were spurred to action when we discovered that many children did not have a single book of their own. We built bookshelves and filled them with brand new books for a local children's shelter. When we went to deliver the bookshelves we were shocked and dismayed that the only response we got was "Put them over there." We had imagined delighted children eager to read the books, not grumpy adults on the take. Rather than being discouraged we talked to community leaders about our hopes for the project. They encouraged us to visit schools. We contacted ten local schools identified as "low income." Of these ten schools one principal agreed to let us come in and read to the children and let them pick out a brand new book. We learned a lot on our first visits. We added nameplates with the children's name on them, and started showing off our library cards and telling the children about the public library. Our friends joined us and started acting out the stories as they were read. We were encouraged by the smiles and laughter of the children. We continued to contact schools and tell them about our program. It took a lot of persistence. Not many principals or teachers could understand teens wanting to visit K-3rd grade classrooms to read and give out books. We persisted. We also wrote hundreds of letters to publishers, authors, and bookstores searching for books. Our rate of return was dismal. BUT: we slowly gathered support. And it was much

> "Feel the fear and do it anyway."
> ~ Susan Jeffers

like a snowball rolling downhill. As our program became more successful, more folks wanted to be a part of it, give books, support the program, and volunteer. We started off with the goal of distributing 750 books. To date we've given out more than 24,000 nationwide. What started as a program to read to children and spread the joy of reading has now branched out to a program where a cross culture of teens are involved in learning important skills like time management, public speaking, and organization as they help less fortunate children.

Unfortunately, we continue to have to work hard to spread the joy of reading. It gets easier but we've found you cannot let up on the effort needed to keep the program alive. We invent opportunities to spread the joy of reading by declaring "National Share the Joy of Reading Month" and speaking to service clubs. We blog. We write letters. We pester friends to join in. Our program is successful but "to whom much is given, much is expected." We must continue to develop the program. Along the way we fine-tune and improve the program. We weigh opportunities based on effort versus benefits...and then we remember our true purpose: helping less fortunate children learn that reading is fun. Having a book of your very own that you picked out is a wonderful treat. And we remember the smiles, the children hugging their books and then we know we must persist on: write more letters, tell more folks and set up more events. It is easier to persist when you believe in your cause and you are making a positive difference. We hope to spark others with this cause so that more will take part in the journey. We know that to persist you must have a vision of what you want to accomplish. For us it was to share the joy of reading directly with less fortunate children. You must also set goals. This helps inspire you and keep you on track. We are constantly setting new goals for our program: either in terms of books given out, events planned or volunteers recruited. You must also be passionate about your project. We write so many letters, grant requests, and calls to action. Our return rate is wretched. However, rather than focus on the negative, we work with the folks that call or write back. We do what we can with what we have. And we celebrate our successes. At each milestone, we make sure our supporters know of our success. This winter we competed in a contest for $10,000. It took a community of help to win and we made sure to thank our supporters. We've learned that our supporters need to be encouraged to be persistent as well. And the benefit? The smile of the children as they hug their books. And the little kid that points you out to his family as one of the book kids who gave him that book he really, really, really loves. Then we know that the many efforts we continue to make are worth it.

About Kyle and Brady Baldwin

Kyle and Brady Baldwin are brothers from Northern California who started a non-profit organization, My Own Book, to share the joy of reading with less fortunate children. They send teams of teens to visit K-3rd grade classrooms to read a story, tell about the public library, and then let the children pick a brand new book of their very own. Finally, a personalized bookplate is added to each book. They are always looking for volunteers. More information about My Own Book and volunteer opportunities can be found at www.myownbook.net.

Dare to Make a Difference by Randi Smith-Todorowski

People come into our lives for a reason, a season or a lifetime. Sometimes it takes years to truly appreciate the lessons different people have to teach us.

Teachers come in all shapes and sizes.

Jack has taught me:
- Clearly defined goals reap clearly defined results.
- Speaking louder doesn't clarify my message, only exposes my frustrations.
- It really is about the journey.
- Negative reinforcement crushes enthusiasm.
- Mix belief, commitment, patience and enthusiasm and miracles happen.

Jack is 6. He has autism. Just over a year ago, his Dad brought him in for lessons. He greeted me with a hug and held on so tight that he slid down my leg taking my elastic-waist kung fu pants with him. At that moment, I knew I couldn't put him in the regular group lesson and I knew I couldn't send him away.

At 5, Jack could not sit still, follow directions, balance without leaning or even control his saliva. He was going to force me to grow as a teacher. After a year of private lessons, today he can do push ups, sit ups, catch and throw and even link a series of movements together to demonstrate the Tiger short form. However, the greatest news of this story is that in the fall he will be attending public school for the first time with his twin sister. I cannot take credit for this accomplishment, but am proud to be a part of this miracle. Earlier this month, I was the recipient of the NAWBO Phoenix Unsung Hero Award. I was proud to be recognized publicly, by my peers for my persistent efforts in helping other women to grow their businesses. However, the internal reward that comes from personal satisfaction in helping Jack learn to use his body is priceless.

With belief, commitment and persistence, you can start making a difference and creating your own miracles! The giant oak is an acorn that held its ground. Just as an acorn is able to reach its greatest potential by defying all odds and staying firm, we all have the ability to do the same. As Peter Walsh, so boldly states, "Dream Big and Dream Often." Start with self-awareness. You must have a clear vision. The only person who will get you where you want to be is you. What does your giant oak tree look like? Do you wish to be a Broadway dancer, a professional athlete, philanthropist, teacher, stay at-home mom, successful entrepreneur, reality TV show contestant or just a happier person? Begin with the end in mind.

Statistics indicate that one out of 1000 white belts become black belts. I would venture to say it is the ones who begin with the end in mind. Certainly it is those who persist. A Black Belt is not something that you can buy or wear. It is who you become. It is the absolute manifestation of making the seemingly impossible, possible. Black Belt is an attitude. It is a way of life.

Martial art training is an amazing way to develop discipline, experience goal setting and an appreciation for practicing something over and over. I think it is important to recognize individuals and entities that possess that same diligence as having a Black Belt attitude in life and as being are all the oak tree they can be.

I love the story of Tony Hsieh. He helped start,

Zappos.com. In 2008, Zappos booked $1 billion in gross sales. Today the idea of selling shoes online is thought unoriginal. However, in 1999, only 10 years ago, investors were quick to pass on this idea, denouncing there was no evidence it would work. I repeat, in 2008, Zappos booked $1BILLION in gross sales. Clearly he had a vision and held his ground.

Each day we risk being thrown off course by negative thinking, doomsayers, distractions and other people's problems and opinions. Unless, of course, you have a Black Belt In Life Attitude; you are so clear and focused on your vision that nothing stands in your way.

Last year in an effort to make the world a better place, we launched Atlas Online and introduced the idea of distance learning Kung Fu. Just like Zappos, our idea was beat down by traditional thinkers. Although, we can transmit information at warp speeds and earn an MBA online, we were told our idea would never work. Today, we are proud to have global presence and help others feel better, look better and live better around the world. What began as tutorial-streamed videos has blossomed into full online certifications. Looking at an acorn for the first time, you would never imagine its potential. Do you know yours? Does the stuff you do today, help you create the life you want? You can read about vision boards, positive thinking, laws of attraction and manifesting what you want, or you can take action and make it happen!

Be the acorn that becomes the giant oak. Don't wait for next year to try again, games are won and lost in the 2nd half. Make this year the year that you empower your dreams! Create your own legacy. Become a legend in your own mind. Accept a project and pour your heart into it. You will be amazed!

All great things come from a seed, tangible or intangible. As the Chinese proverb goes-The best time to plant a tree is 20 years ago. The second best time is now. If Jack can attend public school, an acorn can become a giant oak tree, an online shoe company can gross over $1 Billion a year and martial arts can be learned online, you can develop the tenacity to reach your dreams. As the saying goes: "persistence wears down resistance."

About Randi Smith-Todorowski

RANDI SMITH-TODOROWSKI, 3rd Degree Black Belt Martial Artist. As a writer, speaker, and Creator of the Premier virtual Kung Fu Academy, Randi has global influence training, teaching and applying the principles of Kung Fu to business success and life. Randi's Kung Fu school in Scottsdale, Arizona has been featured on NBC and is employed by Fortune 500 companies for Self-Defense, Corporate Wellness workshops and Team Building classes. Randi is motivated and inspired to help as many people as she can to reach their greatest potential. Her passion is rooted in helping others to see things in a brighter light and to be comfortable and genuine in the skin they are in. She is also a Certified Yoga Instructor who incorporates martial arts philosophy into her teachings. For more information visit www.atlasmartialarts.com

When you start a business you have to be persistent. by James T. White

When you start a business you have to be persistent. When you start a business at 12 you have to be more persistent. I've always been a businessman. As a child I resold penny candy out of my parents' basement. When I was 12 I used my babysitting money to buy a snow shovel. I went to every house in my neighborhood offering monthly snow removal services for a flat fee. Luckily for me it didn't snow a lot that month but I made enough money to buy a snow blower. It was a good thing, too, because the next month brought a heavy blanket of snow and I spent a lot of time out in the cold pushing my snow blower up and down more and more of my neighbors' driveways. I had no credit and everything I acquired for my business had to be bought with cash. I learned very quickly that it's a lot better to own your equipment out right—always try to have an asset rather than a liability mired down in debt.

I was managing almost 300 people by the time I turned 16. We expanded from snow removal into landscaping and were busy year round. Other kids in my high school worried about exams and crushes. I was worried about exams too—I barely had time to show up for class, let alone study. I knew I could just walk away and maybe get my GED later. But I knew that I needed to prove to myself that I could handle running J & W Lawn Care and Snow Removal Services and being a teenager at the same time. I sold my company the same year I graduated. It was like I had graduated from the business as well. I moved on and found new and bigger ventures.

Always start small. I think that if you don't understand what your employees are doing and what challenges face them, you'll never really be able to understand your own business. I wanted to start a long haul trucking business. I had just sold my company and I had the capital to buy a few trucks and hire some drivers. Instead I bought one truck and I drove it myself. It was hard work and by the time I started working entirely out of the office I knew exactly what those guys were doing every day. It was hard work and I didn't always enjoy it but I'm glad I took the time to learn what my employees were doing because I was able to take that experience back into the office and make sure that I was doing everything I could to keep my employees on time, on track and safe.

My teens were dedicated to persistence. I had to be because it proved to my clients and employees that I took my job seriously and in turn would do the best I could for them. I never had to test my true perseverance until my early twenties.

I've always been a trusting person. I want to believe that at his or her core, every person is good. For the most part I've attracted amazing people and still am in contact with many of the people who I met when I first started out over ten years ago. But in my early twenties I was running a rapidly expanding payday loan company and I surrounded myself with the wrong kind of people. I will never forget the day in October 2007 when I walked into a meeting and learned my CFO had been quietly funneling almost a million dollars out of my clients' trust accounts. I stood there with my mouth hanging open and finally my assistant and best friend took my arm and led me to a seat. In a strange way I didn't care about the money, I cared that I had let people down. I've always been proud of my ability to deliver to my clients and for the first time I knew I wouldn't be able to.

It was a devastating blow but I struggled through with the help of my best friend. He was an incredible support and even now I feel grateful for having had him in my life at that time. My gratitude to him ended the day I asked him to drive my leased car back to the dealership and I never saw the car or him again. Slow details started to leak from everyone who knew him and on top of the failure of my company I learned that the man I thought was my best friend had been playing me for a patsy. December 2008 was a dark time and I was sliding into a deep depression I didn't know how to climb out of. For the first time in nine years I had no job to wake up to in the morning. My company was out of my hands, I had lost my best friend and the global recession was making any attempt to rebuild myself doubly difficult.

To be honest, I don't remember a lot of early 2009. I didn't know what to do with myself and I spent most of my time asleep and the rest in my living watching TV. It all melds together in my mind into one big blur of dark rooms and talking heads floating across the screen.

And then I persisted. I looked at what I loved and what impelled me to get out of bed before this crisis. It was business. I have always loved business and I will always love business. So I threw myself back into the corporate world.

One thing I learned while running my payday lending company was that payday lending is not the way to help people. There is a Chinese proverb that says, give a man a fish and you'll feed him for a day. Teach a man to fish and you feed him for a lifetime. Payday lending just perpetuates the cycle of poverty. I was inspired to actually help people and so I started Texcan Capital Inc. My company is dedicated to helping individuals invest directly in the small businesses in their communities. I realized that at the end of the day, it's the small businesses that are the core of a strong economy and the heart of their communities. Having started and run small businesses my entire life I am now dedicated to helping other individuals do the same.

My love for my companies and the people I meet through them is what gives me my drive and gets me out of bed in the morning. I'm proud to write this on the eve of a new business venture going live. My good friend Stephen Preston runs a design and marketing company focused on small business called PrestonWhite Companies. He offered me the chance to work with him to help foster small business. Stephen believes that the future of all industry is dependent on state of the art web design and cutting edge marketing. I am now helping to finance his customers at low interest rates to help them get the visibility they need while easing the strain on cash flow that visibility previously would have caused. I'm excited to be moving forward and taking my enthusiasm and, yes, my persistence to many different businesspeople and to help small businesses all over North America succeed.

At the end of the day we all have to remember that all of us will face challenges in our lives. Some are minor and some are major. But those challenges are our stories. They shape who we are and who we want to be. All of us have the ability to be persistent. Our lives are persistence. Our stories are our persistence. Look back on your own story and your own challenges; your own perseverance. Each of us has in us the ability to tackle the challenges in our lives, to be persistent and ultimately to succeed.

About James Timothy White
James Timothy White is a businessman and entrepreneur. He is CEO of Texcan Capital Inc. (http://www.texcancapital.com)

and works with PrestonWhite Companies
(http://www.prestonwhitecompanies.com). He is author of
five books including his new release, *Going Public: 31 Essential
Tips from the Kid Millionaire on a Personal Journey* and is a
motivational speaker. He was born in Calgary, Alberta and
splits his time between Calgary and San Antonio, Texas. More
information about James can be found at
http://www.jamestimothywhite.com.

"Destiny is not a matter of chance,
it is a matter of choice. It is not
something to be waited for, but
rather something to be achieved."
~ William Jenning Bryan

The key to unlocking your dreams is to write them down by Bill Starr

"So Bill, tell us something good that will inspire our listeners!" The question from internationally known media host Montel Williams brought a smile to my face. I was really enjoying my first time on national radio and Montel was really pumped about My Life List. (www.mylifelist.org). I proceeded to share how creating a life list and taking action on just one goal will create a sequence of events that will significantly improve your life.

Soon after the show ended, I spoke on the phone with the producer. She was very happy with the segment and thanked me for creating my company, for doing what I have chosen to do with my life. I was touched, and when I hung up, I started to reflect on all that had happened to get me to this point.

Two years earlier, I had left my healthy six-figure investment banking job in Sydney, Australia, to launch a company to develop the My Life List brand and the "create, act, celebrate" goal-achievement methodology. Personally, I was an avid life lister, having ticked off a few life list goals over the years, such as going to college, qualifying as a chartered accountant, living in four different countries, climbing Mt. Kilimanjaro, scuba diving the Great Barrier Reef, and most recently, completing a Sydney Hobart Ocean Race aboard a Volvo 60 round-the-world yacht. But one thing missing from my list of achievements was running my own business. I was constantly thinking about my passions and the type of business I would like to start.

I had heard about the concept of creating a life list after reading about John Goddard in the first *Chicken Soup for the Soul* book. At the age of 15, Goddard wrote at the top of a yellow note pad the three words "My Life List" and wrote a list of 127 goals. John is now in his 80s and has accomplished 109 of the original 127 goals. He often is referred to as the "real-life Indiana Jones" and is considered the world's greatest goal achiever, having accomplished more than 400 goals.

> "Its never that you are not good enough, its just that you could always be better."
> Rachel Kenny

When a friend called with the idea to build a business around the life list concept, I jumped at the chance. It was a great opportunity, to inspire people and enable them to accomplish their goals. After 18 months of research and development, we launched the award-winning goal achievement website (www.mylifelist.org) on Jan. 1, 2009. The site was very well received and the feedback was positive despite this being Phase 1 of our release. With that said, the feeling of accomplishment was unbelievable for me.

Only I know how close I was to walking away and giving up on my goal to make My Life List a success. The six months leading up to the launch were incredibly challenging, as I overcame a series of events that delayed the launch and nearly derailed the whole business.

The first occurred after I returned from completing the Newport Bermuda Ocean Race, which was one of my life list goals. My business partner picked me up at the airport and I could sense something was wrong. We sat down together and he told me that our partnership was not working for him.

Needless to say, I was stunned. I had contributed all of the capital to get us to this point and I had left my job and moved to Los Angeles to make this happen. We were just starting to build real momentum and now he no longer wanted to be in business together. I was shocked and felt like my friend had just thrown a hand grenade into the room and locked the only door.

Thankfully, I had structured the business properly and we were able to come to a financial arrangement by which I would continue to own the business and he would go onto other projects. The negative impact of this was massive. Not only was I financially stretched, but I also had lost a champion for the business and most devastatingly, a best friend.

The next thing that happened was equally as unexpected. After such an emotional negotiation, I decided to return to Canada and find some peace at my 20-year high school reunion (another life list goal). This was exactly the recharge I needed and I was very excited to get back to LA and continue my work. Unfortunately, when I reached the border, I was refused re-entry to the United States. As a Canadian, you are allowed to stay in the United States for six months at a time as a visitor without a visa. While we were building the website, I was making no money and didn't think I needed a work visa. I was spending my money on a venture and was not effectively employed by anyone. As the sole managing partner, with the website about to launch, I decided it was time to get a U.S. work visa at the border.

As a Canadian chartered accountant, I was eligible for a one-year visa (TN), which can be issued by U.S. Immigration officials at the airport. Unfortunately I missed the part that said, "You are unable to get a visa for a company for which you are the majority shareholder." With that, they refused me entry at the border, which is quite serious and can result in a five-year ban from entering the United States. The immigration officer was initially upset with me but soon realized I was making an honest mistake and allowed me to withdraw my visa application without a ban. This was a relief but now I was stranded in Canada with no way to return to my work in LA.

Even though I was not banned, I no longer had proper cause to enter the United States now that they knew I was carrying on business without a proper work visa. I spent a week working this one out and soon contacted a lawyer to help me. It turned out that the visa I should have applied for was the Business Investor Visa (E2). The lawyers reviewed my case and for $5,000 they were able to help me get a five-year work visa. By this time, I was out of money and was forced to borrow money from my life insurance policy. It took a few weeks but I was allowed back into the United States for a month to get the documents I needed to file for my visa. This was so frustrating because I wasn't able to focus on the business at all, and the My Life List site launch was delayed again. The great irony was that I was launching a goal achievement website and crashing into major financial and emotional barriers of my own in the process. I was seriously bending and close to breaking but I knew from all the research I had done on goal achievement that this was a key moment. I was at the point of no return and I needed to make a decision. I could give up or achieve something of significance in my life that I would be proud of, that would serve to inspire others.

One of the key principles of the My Life List methodology is to celebrate significant life experiences by sharing stories that will inspire others. Sharing these stories also helps us to remember when we overcame significant barriers to accomplish a major life goal. The Celebration story that I look to for inspiration is when I climbed Mount Kilimanjaro in Africa. The Summit Push was the most challenging experience I had ever encountered as we climbed straight up for six hours from 16,000 feet to 21,000 feet in the middle of the night.

I had never been through a more taxing physical or mental challenge as we shuffled up that mountain face in the dark. I actually felt I had no choice but to go up. To go down was too dangerous and to stop meant I would freeze, so the only option was up. We continued to the summit and I'm proud to say I have watched the sun rise from the highest point in Africa. I found a determination and persistence within me that night that I look to whenever I am facing a major challenge that I need to overcome.

Getting the site to launch and the events of the six months before launch were merely barriers that I needed to overcome. I found a way forward by finding my inner strength and by enrolling others to support me. Taking action on this life list goal has certainly created a sequence of events that has significantly improved my life. I now have created something of which I am extremely proud and I know mylifelist.org helps people to accomplish their goals. If you have a dream locked away, write it down to get the key for achieving it!

About Bill Starr
Bill Starr is an avid "life lister" and a founding partner and CEO of My Life List (www.mylifelist.org), an award-winning goal achievement website that uses a proven methodology and the power of social networking to help people achieve their goals and inspire others.

How I got fired four times and still made it to The White House by John Follis

In the ad biz they say you can't be any good if you haven't been fired. Well, I'm obviously very good then.

Ad people do get canned more than most -- it's an industry thing. Nevertheless, four times is a lot and each was a painful experience casting mounting doubts about my talent and career. Unbeknownst to me at the time those firings set me on course that led to my co-founding an award-winning Madison Avenue ad agency and being honored at The White House. But after firing number three things weren't looking good. No one, and I mean no one, would talk to me. Even the headhunters wouldn't return my calls. Not able to get any interviews with the agencies I knew, I began going through the phonebook calling those I didn't. One day I made 106 calls and got 104 rejections.

One of those calls got me a meeting with an agency exec who said he was extremely impressed with my work. Though I'd gotten that positive response quite a bit (whenever I was actually able to get people to see my work) I'd been around long enough to be wary of flattering words and promises to "call" when something came up. So, when weeks turned into months, and the call never came, I wasn't surprised.

When the phone rang two years later, and it was that same guy calling about a possible project, I was shocked. That call eventually led to a meeting, which eventually led to a collaboration, which eventually resulted in some of the most exciting, successful work I'd ever done in my career. Up to that point my career I had been struggling to keep a job. Suddenly, I was part of one of the most talked about campaigns in the city, for Kenneth Cole. Awards and press quickly followed. It also attracted a smooth-talking, dark-suited business guy who was convinced that he and I should team up and start the next great NY ad agency. Intrigued, but certainly not convinced of anything, I began a collaboration, and within a year we had a small agency that began winning business, awards and great press. Who knew?

It was during this time that I, independently, created one of my best ads ever - an anti-child abuse ad that got my partner very excited. Determined to find an organization to run it we managed to get a meeting with people at the National Committee for the Prevention of Child Abuse who just happened to be planning a visit to New York from Chicago. It was a lucky break since, without a face-to-face meeting, our chances of selling our ad were slim to none. When our big moment came and we revealed our ad, the NCPCA folks could not have been less excited. They felt it was way too controversial. But, they were excited enough about us to give us a great project: a great national TV assignment! I'm proud to say that the campaign we eventually created contributed to a 57% increase in abuse hotline calls, won some major awards, and got great press.

It was shortly thereafter that I received a curious letter with the words, THE WHITE HOUSE as the return address. Considering the many creative job seekers who were now vying for my attention as a potential employer, I assumed it was yet another gimmicky attempt to simply grab my attention. To my utter amazement it turned out to be, in fact, an actual invitation for a White House gala honoring those select few whose public service contributions had "made a positive difference." A couple weeks later, there I was. That White House experience is something I will never forget.

It is also a story I don't mind sharing. Because if someone had told me that after being fired four times I'd have my own award-winning, Madison Avenue ad agency and be honored at The White House, I would have said, "you should get off the meds."

I've heard it said that hard things get put in our way, not to stop us, but to call out our courage and strength. Though I'm not sure how much courage and strength played a part in this story, I've at least always tried to keep up my hopes. So, if this story helps you with that, then I'm happy to have shared it with you.

About John Follis
John Follis is President/Creative Director of Follis Advertising, an award-winning advertising/marketing firm. Before Follis Advertising, John was co-founder of Follis DeVito Verdi, one of Madison Avenue's most awarded agencies. John is also a contributing columnist for ADWEEK and a nationally published essayist. A requested speaker on effective marketing and Social Media, he has also contributed his marketing talents to two dozen charitable causes, including Child Abuse Prevention, for which he was honored at The White House. He also hosts his own marketing podcast, The Marketing Show, and is one of the few ad men profiled on Wikipedia. He can be reached at john@follisinc.com

Power of Persistence By Sima Sorensen

It was February 2007. I remember it so clearly because it was the day that changed my life. Up until this point my life was far from what I had I imagined for myself.

I was a divorced, single mom living in Los Angeles with my six-year old daughter. I wasn't receiving child support and my income as a personal trainer was so little that I didn't have enough money to pay my rent. I felt scared and alone. My family was back home in Israel, so I had no support system here in the U.S. I had to make a change. I knew that I needed to get more clients, but I also needed to somehow make a connection with a person of power; someone who would appreciate my talents and open the door to more opportunities for me. I wouldn't ask them for money, just that they allow me to work with them. I knew that if I gave them my 110% the money would follow. This is a philosophy of mine that I believe developed in my early years in Israel. At the age of eleven I left my family to live in a kibbutz; a collective community that would provide me shelter, food and clothing, in exchange for work on the farm. But that's a whole other story.

I had heard one of my friends talking about a hotel owner, real estate mogul, and bank owner that he was working with. For the sake of privacy, I will refer to him as "mogul". I knew of this man and imagined how busy and stressed he must be in his day-to-day business, and I knew I could help him. So I asked my friend for his number. He was reluctant to give it to me, but I was persistent. After making me swear on the Torah that I would not reveal how I obtained the moguls personal number, he finally relinquished.

I called the mogul the next day and told him that I would love to work with him and offer my services as a personal trainer, food and life coach. He listened for about twenty-five seconds before saying "How did you get my number? Don't call me again!" and he hung up. It wasn't the nicest exchange, but I expected that. I picked up the phone and called him back. "I think we had bad reception", I explained. "No" he said, "I hung up on you". "OK", I said to him. "I understand, but I'm not asking for anything, I just want to give you the gift of a healthy life." "Do not call me back", he stated and hung up on me once again. I had a strong feeling that he would end up calling me back, so I left it alone and did not try to contact him again. The very next day he called and gave me his assistant's phone number! "Call Candy, and tell her to give you fifteen minutes with me. No more".

I called his assistant and scheduled an appointment three weeks down the road. I waited patiently for that day to come. Right before our scheduled date his assistant called and said "We have to reschedule". I wasn't going to give up, so I made an appointment for the following week. I knew that this man was very busy, under extreme pressure, and that he needed my help.

> "Challenges are what make life interesting; overcoming them is what makes life meaningful."
> ~Joshua J. Marine

The day finally arrived and I could hardly contain my happiness as I drove down the 405 freeway. I arrived thirty minutes early. It is my belief that you never arrive with empty hands. In researching this man I discovered that he was religious, so I arrived with a gift for him, a small bible. People don't expect small tokens like this, and it takes them pleasantly by surprise. In his mind he was probably expecting me to ask for a hand out, but once I presented him with my gift, he seemed to relax. I was looking for an opportunity, not charity. "Candy, get us some water, close the door, and forward my calls", the mogul ordered. I knew I had won him over. Our "fifteen minute" meeting turned into one and a half hours. I told him that I wasn't asking for money, and that I would offer my services free of charge for the opportunity to work with him. In my experience you reap many more rewards by giving to people, rather than asking and taking. He agreed to work with me as a client, and we booked our first session.

For our first training session I came to his office and insisted that his cell phone be out of the room with his assistant. He was a powerful businessman, but I was persistent and was going to treat him the same way I do all my clients. And he listened. Everybody was SHOCKED as the mogul is obsessed with his phone and probably gets twenty calls a minute. I knew that was the first major step in helping the mogul with his health. We discussed his food plan, and he wrote down everything I said. At the end of the session, he gave me his home address and asked if I would come to train him and his wife. I didn't charge him for that first session, which in turn gave him the opportunity to help me. He ended up referring me to more than fifty clients! The mogul and his referrals helped me build my business, get my life back on track, and introduced me to many important people in my life. He became my mentor, and I his. The mogul is still in my life to this day.

No matter what they say or how many times they say no to you, never give up. Try a different approach. Go from above, under, the left and then the right, until that "no" turns into a "yes". I was and am persistent not only for myself, but more importantly for my daughter, and proud of it!

About Sima Sorensen

Sima Sorensen was born and raised in Tel Aviv, Israel. At 18 she joined the Israeli Army as a fitness sergeant. Two years later in 1991 she moved to Los Angeles and became a certified personal trainer and instructor. She has worked at some of the top gyms in the U.S. including Bally and L.A. Fitness. Sima has competed in numerous fitness competitions around the country and has won many titles including, "Ms.Venice Beach" and "Ms .Fitness Palm Springs". It is her goal to assist her clients in achieving a more balanced life through fitness, nutrition and overall healthy living. Sima is not only a dedicated trainer, food and life coach, but a loving mother and community volunteer. Sima is currently living happily in CA where she trains clients at her Sherman Oaks studio and all over southern California, is raising her daughter and building her "Red Carpet Fit" empire. For More Information visit: Http://redcarpetfit.com

"If at first you don't succeed, try try again."
~W. C. Fields

Setting the Goal for Olympic Gold by Tim Morehouse

My eyes are fixed upon Keeth Smart, anchor of the United States Men's Saber Fencing Team, as he darts back and forth, battling Russia's Stanislav Pozniakov in the semi-final Men's Saber Fencing match at the 2008 Olympics in Beijing, China. Russia holds a five-point lead over the United States. Pozniakov is not merely a member of the Russian fencing team; he is the best anchor in the world – the Mariano Rivera of fencing.

I am one of the four members of the United States Men's Saber Fencing Team, and as Keeth's match with Pozniakov progresses, I am increasingly struck with a sense of déjà vu. Four years before, at the 2004 Olympic Games in Athens, Keeth had battled Pozniakov to a score of 44-44. Team USA's hopes to leave Athens with a medal in men's saber fencing hung in the balance. Yet, on the match's final point, Keeth and Pozniakov simultaneously lunged towards each other, striking at the same time. Our fate lay in the hands of the referee. The seconds felt like hours as we waited. The referee awarded the point to the Russians, and at once we felt the weight of our defeat. We returned home with nothing.

Now, as I watch Keeth and Pozniakov, I notice the score has begun to resemble Athens more and more. Keeth continues to chip away at the Russian advantage: 36-41, 38-42, 41-43. My heart pounds in suspense and excitement as the match goes on. And then: 44-44. It's like Athens all over again. I kneel down and hold my teammates' hands, just as we had done four years earlier. My nerves race and my mind reels. We are on the precipice of achieving what no U.S. Men's Saber team has done since 1948, returning home with an Olympic medal – and I'm not even supposed to be here.

In fact, I was never supposed to be on an Olympic team at all. My ascent through the ranks of the fencing world, and my seat next to Jason Rogers, James Williams, and Keeth Smart on Team USA, is an unlikely story. No one has ever called me a natural fencer. I have never possessed the graceful, traditional form of most elite fencers. Nor had I ever achieved any level of dominance in the sport until college. My success is the product of an inner determination, a refusal to listen to the general consensus: that I would never make it in the sport of fencing.

*****

I began to fence on a whim, at age thirteen, as a way to get out of gym class. I took to the sport mainly because it gave my best friend Ying and I a chance to hit each other with swords without getting in trouble. I often arrived late to practice and I didn't exhibit any noticeable skill in the sport. It was not the most auspicious of beginnings.

I had arrived at Riverdale Country School, an elite private school in New York City, from a public school in Harlem. I struggled in my new school, receiving Cs or below in my classes. Worse, during my time on the fencing team I had attracted a bully named Bell. He was seventeen, a junior at the high school, and a physical giant in my thirteen-year-old eyes. He began with verbal abuse, avoiding the coach's attention, but making sure I understood how little he thought of me and how much he wanted me off the team. The combination of Bell's constant abuse and my academic struggles became an increasingly heavy burden. I wondered if something was wrong with me. Perhaps I deserved this treatment?

I went to practice sporadically and without any enthusiasm. Then one day, the coach called me aside and said something unexpected. "I believe in you." He told me that I had potential as a fencer. For the first time someone at my new school was telling me that I could succeed. But he followed with, "If you miss any more practices we're going to cut you."

Encouraged by my coach, I began to show up every day on time, and listen to his instructions. Yet, Bell's abuse continued, growing harsher and more violent. And one day I found myself running in the cold of winter, sweat bursting from my brow and streaming down my body. Bell's giant figure loomed behind me as he wielded a fencing blade and forced me to run laps. When I collapsed from exhaustion he whipped the blade down upon my back. As we returned back to the fencing room, Bell suddenly grabbed me and pushed me into an alley, holding me against the wall. "I want you to quit! You are a waste and you'll never be any good. I don't want you to come back to the fencing room ever again," he growled. He then walked away, leaving me alone. I walked into the locker room and wept aloud.

Standing between the lockers, I thought seriously about quitting. The torment and struggles seemed too much to bear. Yet, in that moment I remembered my coach's encouragement, "You can be good, I believe in you." These words suddenly solidified in my mind, and I resolved not only to continue to fence in the face of Bell's insults and assaults, but to continue fencing despite any obstacle that appeared in my path. It was a decision that permanently influenced my fencing career and my attitude towards life as well. Instead of quitting the team, I began to practice with increasing rigor. I aimed to compete in a small, local high school tournament, the Mamaroneck Invitation. By senior year, I became the Mamaroneck champion.

Despite my local success, I was far from a rising star in the fencing world. Only one college, Brandeis University, recruited me. None of the major powerhouses had even glanced my way. Nevertheless, spurred on by my determination to succeed, I set my sights on a seemingly unrealistic goal: *to become a first team All-American.* I did not even qualify for the championships my freshman year. My form was awkward and I employed my own unique maneuvers that flew in the face of fencing's traditional moves. Yet, I continued to practice and to chip away at my goal - point-by-point and match-by-match. I spent long days in the training room, my muscles aching from thousands of lunges, advances, and retreats. Just as it had in high school, my work paid off. I graduated Brandeis in 2000-ranked 18th in United States, having become a three-time All-American fencer and only the second All-American in Brandeis' history.

Still, I had plenty of doubters. And I still possessed my clumsy form and unconventional moves. Most members of the fencing community considered my success a fluke. It was commonly believed that I had "overachieved" during college. So I was not on anyone's radar to arrive in Athens during the summer of 2004 as a member of the U.S. Men's Saber Fencing Team. Yet, that is exactly what I resolved to do: *to make the Olympic team.*

The obstacles lying on the road to Athens were as numerous as they were daunting. There are only four spots on the U.S. men's fencing team. The fourteen fencers who stood between me and a trip to Athens were the most skilled and formidable in the nation. They had trained at elite academies, practiced and mastered fencing's most difficult techniques, and were several years younger than I. Many of them also possessed another asset that I lacked, funding.

Lacking the visibility of other Olympic sports, such as swimming and figure skating, corporate sponsorship of aspiring Olympic fencers is unheard of in the United States. Those of us determined to compete on the Olympic stage are forced to foot the entire bill ourselves. In the pursuit of my dream the expenses piled up. As I traveled to Europe, South America, and Asia to compete and work my way up in the rankings, I repeated the same phrase over and over, "Put it on the card, on the card on the card..." These trips, my coach's fees, my gym memberships, and my equipment were all financed by my credit card. In the end, I went $30,000 in debt for the mere *chance* to fulfill my Olympic dream.

If that was not enough, I was working full time. Inspired by a radio program featuring education pioneer, Wendy Kopp, I had joined Teach For America, an organization that recruits talented college graduates and places them in country's toughest and most impoverished schools. Teach For America, has been a tremendous success, continually improving failing schools despite the odds. The program had many skeptics. I felt a kinship.

And so between the hours before dawn, when I would wake up bleary eyed and head to the training room, and the hours after dusk, when I would resume my practice regime, I stood at the front of a classroom of thirty low-income students, pushing them to catch up to their upper-income peers. As I learned about their lives and their struggles, I found myself echoing the words of my Coach, the words I repeated way back when I sat in that empty locker room, crying and ready to quit. I let my students know that no obstacle or fear is insurmountable if you summon your will to succeed. I showed the kids in my class that the biggest failure of all is the failure to try – not going for it and making justifications why you couldn't, or wouldn't, or shouldn't. I did not want to be a role model for my kids but an inspiration to them. My experience in the classroom, teaching and learning from some of the most disadvantaged students in the nation, renewed and strengthened my commitment to persevere. The power of belief and faith in the self had never been clearer.

With such thoughts in mind I plunged into my training and pursuit of my Olympic dream with even greater enthusiasm than before. As I trained and pressed on I received a few lucky breaks. Of the fourteen fencers standing between me and a spot on the Olympic team, almost half gave up. Yet, my leap forward in the standings did little to dispel the fencing community's doubts and pessimism regarding my chances. My success was still regarded as a fluke, and I was still seen as someone who had reached beyond my capabilities. My fall was considered inevitable and imminent.

Instead, I walled out the negativity, focused on my dream, and sweated past my remaining competition to win a place on Team USA's Men's Saber Fencing team as the alternate, the team's fourth member. I took time to revel in my success, proud of my accomplishments. Yet, I knew the greatest task lay ahead of me. A new goal formed the moment that I had achieved my last: *to win in Athens*. There was still a lot of fighting left to do.

I trained with my teammates with a ferocious intensity and drive. Although I did not compete, my teammates made me feel that I was as much a part of the team as the ones who were out on the strip. Their triumphs were my triumphs, their defeats my defeats. We were one team, bound together and struggling with a common purpose. We entered our first match surrounded by a sentiment that I had become all too familiar with. Nobody in the fencing community expected us to succeed. Compared to other nations, whose fencing teams are both extremely popular and extremely well funded, we were the clear underdogs. When we defeated Hungary in the opening round a nation was sent reeling. The Hungarian figureheads, furious and embarrassed, terminated Hungary's coach, manager, and trainer. Losing to the U.S. team was considered the ultimate in upsets.

Our unlikely success brought us into the second round to face the French. We battled and held our own and our Olympic journey fell into the hands of Keeth Smart. Keeth's closing match went down to the wire and up to a score that would eventually have a striking familiarity to me: 44-44. Sitting on the bench, I prayed, I believed, and made every effort to will Keeth on to victory. Yet, it was not enough. The referee ruled the final point in favor of the French and we were left with only a shot at the bronze.

Then it was the semi-finals, the United States against the Russians, Keeth Smart against Stanislav Pozniakov, 36-41, 38-42, 41-43. 44-44. Then the simultaneous lunges, the unfavorable ruling, the heartbreaking return home; all of this rang in our minds as a new goal crystallized before us: *to win a medal in Beijing* in 2008.

I arrived in Beijing, China as a competing member of team, ready to step onto the strip and fence on the sport's largest stage. The most significant and challenging moment of my fencing career came in the semi-final round as I stood across from Alexey Yakimenko, the young Russian fencer who had been ranked number one in the world the year before. The score was displayed to the world, Russia: 35, USA: 28. The match began and the stadium went black, with only Yakimenko and me illuminated beneath the spotlight. Our match was the eighth of nine in the semi-final round and we would fence until one of us reached 40 points. Our team had suffered defeats in our last four matches and we appeared headed towards defeat. I needed to win. "I came to play today, I came to play today," I repeated to myself.

I was slow out of the gate and Yakimenko struck to increase the Russian lead. I could hear my friends cheer me on as I regained my composure and stared Yakimenko down. We traded points as we danced along the strip, my body moving with a sole purpose, to close the gap and give Keeth Smart a chance. I blocked, parried, reposted. I lunged forward and struck and when the match was over I had scored 7 points, Yakimenko had scored 5. I walked to the bench, my muscles strained and my heart wild with hope and fear.

*****

"It is a funny thing about life: If you refuse to accept anything but the best you very often get it."
~ W. Somerset Maugham

Now, sitting and waiting, I will on my teammate. I shove my fears away and bend my thoughts towards victory. The battle for the final point begins, and I follow Keeth with my eyes as he steps forward, then back, and then he hesitates. My heart stops and I can feel my nerves pulsing. And in this instant Keeth changes his retreat into a forward motion, flying towards Pozniakov with his saber, beating Pozniakov's parry by less than a second. The green light blinks and I hear Keeth release a piercing scream of victory.

I rise from the bench in stunned exhilaration. As I leap towards my teammates, I suddenly begin to fall and the world goes black. When I regain consciousness moments later, I spring up and race towards my teammates. Tears run down our cheeks as we celebrate the victory to which we dedicated our every ounce of life and faith. We will return home to the United States with a medal, the first for the nation since 1948.

For the past four years this moment existed only in my imagination. Yet, as our celebration ends, I look over at the French team, our opponent in the final round – the gold medal round. Their calm composure is striking next to our wild exhilaration. Like us, they too have a goal - to stand at the top of the Olympic podium. When the final round begins we summon our strength, our talent, our drive, and face the French. Despite our effort they defeat us. We will take home the silver medal.

Leaving Athens, I reflect on our victory and our defeat. The high bar we set for ourselves, the distant dream we allowed ourselves to chase, cannot be understated as a critical factor in our success. But why hadn't we set out, like the French did, to win the gold? Perhaps our goal to win an Olympic medal was too small? Would a bigger dream have led to the ultimate prize? It's a lesson that I will now carry with me for a lifetime. And I will also take it to London in 2012. There is no doubt that it's time: *to go for the gold in London.*

About Tim Morehouse

Ranked in the top 5 amongst American fencers and in the top 10 internationally, Tim Morehouse has fought his way to the top of his sport. Tim has harnessed hard work, focus, and talent to forge a unique life as an Olympic silver medalist, motivational speaker, and inspirational teacher. From humble beginnings as a wild kid who was almost kicked off his high school fencing team, Tim has battled past every obstacle standing between him and Olympic glory. He is currently the national spokesperson for Kid Fitness, geared toward helping kids make healthy choices. For more on Tim Morehouse visit www.TimMorehouse.com

Believe in Yourself by Mary Jones

When I was 38 years old, my husband Jim died of a sudden massive heart attack. He had just turned 40, was a high school and college athlete who continued to exercise throughout the years and was in good physical shape.

I owned a corporate recruiting firm at the time. Years later, as I approached my 50th birthday, I began to think seriously about getting into radio. Prior to recruiting, I was Director of a non-profit organization and during those years had recorded public service announcements. I always enjoyed being in the studio and even then thought about pursuing a radio career at some point.

Having always been a goal-oriented person and giving significance to life's milestones, my upcoming 50th birthday was looming large. While I still enjoyed my recruiting business, I longed for the feeling of exhilaration and daily challenge that had faded over the years.

So, a goal was set. It was the end of 2000, and my 50th was November of the next year. I told myself that I would in fact have a talk show by my next birthday.

There were no more than a handful of local talk shows in the Hartford, CT area at the time and I had no connections or contacts within that industry. But, what I did have was determination and commitment. After all, I had set a goal, and the clock was ticking.

I soon realized that I had something else, too. Something that was fueled by my husband's death and that was providing me great encouragement and drive.

I realized that Jim hadn't had a chance to fulfill his dreams, to realize all that he could have been and done in his life. But, I did. And, at that moment, I decided not only to go after my dream with enormous gusto, but...to do it for him. I made a commitment to myself to take full advantage of my life and to make the most of having the opportunity to do so.

> "When I was 5 years old my mom told me happiness was the key to life. In school, they asked what I wanted to be when I grew up. I wrote down "happy." They told me I didn't understand the assignment, I told them they didn't understand life."
> Anonymous

I was able to secure a meeting with the General Manager of a radio station. I pitched my idea of a show on careers- a natural outflow of my recruiting business. I pointed out that there wasn't a program on that topic in the local market, why there should be, and why I should be the person to host it. He was receptive to the idea and asked me to put together a demo tape.

I learned along the way...about mid-year 2001...that the radio industry is like any other industry- it's driven by sales, and sales equates to advertising in radio. So, while figuring out and working on my demo, I discovered that I would also need to bring several advertisers to my show.

As in many things in life, and most goals, when surprises arise that make the process more difficult than initially thought, it's easy to abandon your aspirations. Then, and mostly then, you need to hold onto that which gives you that inner belief in yourself, and the resolve to continue on. It's about persistence.

For me, that persistence re-appeared each time I reminded myself of my commitment to make the absolute most of my life...at least I had the opportunity to do so. Each reminder brought me a renewed sense of energy and excitement about moving forward. Working through and moving past the obstacles then became a fun challenge. Attitude truly makes the difference.

I completed my demo, submitted it and waited for 'the call' ...that call that would tell me I could start my show. I had also secured a couple of advertisers. My 50th birthday was just a week away.

I decided to follow-up with the station GM and placed a call to him three days before my birthday. No callback by my birthday. But, two days later, I heard back...my show would start shortly after the first of the year.

I have now been doing my show for 8 years and loving every moment. After the first year, I switched from focusing on careers to talking about issues of everyday life from a positive perspective.

The need for me to bring in advertisers continued until the show became established and popular. At that point, the station committed its sales staff to selling my show.

One of the things that has always been important to me...even as a young woman...is not to have regrets at the end of my life. There have been a multitude of surveys over the years asking elderly people to reflect back on their lives in an attempt to capture some of their acquired wisdom. Invariably, the responses touch upon not regretting what they did, but what they did not do. My husband's death reinforced that and continues to remind and motivate me.

However, I've learned along the way that while some people have that drive and determination to follow their dreams, goals, and aspirations, it can be fleeting. Wanting something badly is very different than actually making it happen.

That difference, while critical, is also simple. It's being willing to persist.

What has worked for me is to figure out why each dream and goal is important, and what is driving me to fulfill it. More than the goal itself, it's about the motivation for wanting it. For me, it is clear. I want to experience as much as life has to offer, before the time comes when I no longer can. That drive in and of itself gives me the persistence to pursue with vigor those things that I set my sights on.

That drive is different for everyone. And it will vary from time to time, goal to goal. But, before you decide to enlist your time, energy and resources into any pursuit, think about why it's important to you. If the reason isn't one of significance or emotional value, reconsider. Only that will propel you to overcome the obstacles you'll undoubtedly meet along the way. Only that will feed your determination. Dream your dreams, understand your motivations, live life to the fullest and persist until you achieve all you desire.

About Mary Jones
Mary Jones hosts a talk show on WDRC-AM in Hartford, CT and its three-affiliate stations. She is featured on two weekly segments on WVIT NBC TV-30 in CT. Her website is www.maryjonesshow.com.

The Fortune is in the Follow-Up By Kathryn Marion

Making sales (especially for a non-sales person) can really be an uphill battle all the way...especially that very first sale. When I decided to offer content I had from a 15-year-old career, money, and life skills book for new college graduates as single-topic information cards to campus career centers, I placed a call to the career center director at the closest school to my home. It wasn't a sales call because this was, in essence, a new venture—I only asked for some time to discuss the state of counseling today and learn what types of resource materials they had available to students in their office.

The counselor was very gracious with her time and insights, providing me with much excellent information to use in developing my materials. If that was all that came of the meeting, I would have been very happy—I had fulfilled my objective. But, instead, the counselor was very interested in the sample materials I used as visual aids and expressed an interest in getting some for her students. Naturally, I was thrilled to be within reach of a first sale without even trying, but I had no idea how hard I would end up having to work to make it come to fruition.

A few emails were passed back and forth about pricing and sizes of the cards themselves and a purchase order seemed imminent. As I came to realize the huge potential in what I could do with my content, though, I lost track of the amount of time that elapsed between emails...and then they seemed to stop. I wasn't terribly concerned about it and I let even more time pass before following up again. A quick email was sent after a few weeks to see how things were going at their end, with no response (though I didn't notice for another few weeks due to my own busyness).

Another 'quick follow up' to check in again, another weeks long delay with no news, and I finally left a brief voicemail message for the director—again, no response. This went on for many, many months. It was a good thing that I wasn't relying on that potential sale to feed my family! Though I happily got buried in other work, I never completely forgot about this one school.

After *more months* of this, I mentally gave up hope of ever actually seeing a sale from this contact, but I knew I needed to keep on it, especially since the interest they showed in buying from me had been initiated at *their* end in the first place. I posted the advice, *"the fortune is in the follow up"*, above my desk so I would see it each day. Every few weeks I couldn't look at it again without complying, so zipped out another friendly follow-up email or a quick voicemail.

Who knows what was happening in their office during this time—they may have had record numbers of students needing counseling as jobs began to disappear or maybe they lost staff. I'll never know, but I was happy each time my emails did not bounce back and each time I still heard the director's voice on her phone message—at least she was still there and I didn't have to face the prospect of trying to pick up where we left off with new staff.

With all the irons I had in the fire on different projects, I'm sure it would have been very easy to allow even more time to pass between follow-up attempts or maybe to give up altogether. But, 18 months later, after dozens of unanswered emails and voicemail messages, the conversation suddenly started again. First it was apologies from them for being unresponsive for so long...as well as *thanks* for not letting them off the hook (that felt good!). The timing was finally right for them to make a purchase. After several more weeks of emails back and forth to make final product selections and decisions about customization, I had an order in hand—and a good-sized one at that.

This kind of persistence does not come naturally to me, especially when the prize seems likely to be a small one. As far as sales are concerned, I was stepping out of my comfort zone—though in the most comfortable way possible, since *they* initiated the interest in purchasing. But it put the ball firmly in my lap and it was up to me to carry that ball as far and for as long as necessary to reach the goal line, even when I couldn't see it or believed that it may not even exist. I'm sure my weeks-between-contacts method of following up would make professional salesmen cringe, and I certainly don't plan on pursuing *all* sales this way (talk about labor intensive!), but it did prove that saying to be true: the fortune really *is* in the follow-up! So, hang in there and don't drop that ball no matter how long you have to carry it.

About Kathryn Marion
Kathryn Marion is the author of the award-winning book, GRADS: TAKE CHARGE of Your First Year After College! and host of the book's companion resource website, www.GradsTakeCharge.com. She is working on the next book in the Take Charge(tm) series, FRESHMEN: TAKE CHARGE of Your First Year in College! Kathryn is a College-to-Career columnist on Examiner.com, a frequent blog guest, and speaks to high school and college students as well as their parents about success in school and life. She can be found on Twitter, @Tips4Grads, and at www.TakeChargeBookSeries.com.

The Power and Promise of Persistence by Judith Sherven, PhD and Jim Sniechowski, PhD

Persistence is a much-vaunted aspiration. However, in the real world, like dieting, it is not often practiced to its promised benefit.

Persistence carries real promise that can yield real power: not only honing the mental and physical discipline required to live persistence all the way through, but the psychological benefit of a sense of self-esteem that says—"Not only have I done it. I am someone I can trust to do what I say."

Persistence is a psychological feedback mirror in which we get to see who we are and we get to build on what we see.

The Heart of Marketing

Recently our fifth book, *The Heart of Marketing: Love Your Customers and They Will Love You Back,* was published by Morgan James Publishing, 2009. It is the culmination of a five-year journey of persistence that tested and tried us in ways we had never imagined.

In 2000, after seventeen years of practicing therapy, we decided that we needed to reinvent ourselves and, more importantly, reinvent what we were going to do professionally. Whatever it would be it had to be satisfying emotionally, intellectually, and spiritually as well as hold the promise of making the income we were accustomed to.

What we did not expect was the extent of the demand we had placed on ourselves, with no experience or training in sales or marketing much less the Internet.

That leg of our persistence journey lasted just under five years. Five years of determination coupled with many sleepless nights—sleeplessness that resulted from deep surprises as well as the subtle and not so subtle changes we had to go through and integrate before we achieved the first light of clarity as to what might be next.

In 2005 we found ourselves leaping into Internet marketing, a way of life and making a living that in 2000 would have sounded insane had anyone suggested it. But there we were. And the draw toward marketing emerged from somewhere deep inside—a little known cavern of ambition that opened onto a entirely new and foreign vista.

Turning Inside Out

Going from therapy to marketing is not merely changing tasks, it's moving from one dimension of experience into another—with new meanings, new language, new possibilities, new restraints, new skills, a new way of being in the world—a life process that took us from an intense and direct focus on our own inner life and that of our clients to a process that was fundamentally external, tactical, indirect, calculated, and bottom-line driven.

And to get a foothold, with any prospect of success, we thought we had to leave behind the relationship expertise and skills we'd so finely developed. The grief we felt was real and had very much the aura of a death.

That's when we had to either steadfastly hold to our purpose and trust that what we'd fallen into was no accident or accept that we'd made a huge mistake.

Training, Training, Training

We stayed the course and launched into an intense period of training ourselves for this new world. We spared no effort and invested with the high hope that we would learn the world of Internet business and eventually create an income that would surpass what we'd made before. And we would leave the cloister of our offices and make a major presence of ourselves in the wide world.

We'd both earned PhDs but this new study was different, not academic but practical, not merely accumulating information but the need to apply it as quickly as possible. It was a whole new way of learning.

We attended numerous Internet conferences and it was during those conferences that the light of our future began to glow.

> "The difference in the impossible and the possible lies in a persons determination."
> ~Tommy Lasorda

We found ourselves feeling emotionally displaced— out of touch and alien. The hard sell tactics being taught by the purported gurus violated our sense of emotional and spiritual integrity. We soon discovered we were not alone. Many others we spoke with expressed that same displacement. After a while a pattern emerged—those others feeling out of place were all care-givers and service providers—put off by the aggressive, assaultive, even abusive techniques the gurus assured were the stepping stone on the path to wealth and freedom.

For them, perhaps. But not for us and not for those like us. That was when we realized that our relationship skills were central to this evolutionary leap in marketing – a leap in what we call Soft Sell Marketing/.

Soft Sell Marketing

It was out of our displacement and our deep need for a real sense of relationship between seller and buyer that we saw the vision of a new way of marketing. What we came to call soft sell marketing. A marketing style that was respectful of the buyer, and in which the buyer and seller were not in a struggle over who could get the best deal possible.

At that point we produced Bridging Heart and Marketing, our first Internet marketing conference for the soft sell marketers. We were warned against it because the successful Internet marketers could not envision an attendance large enough to prevent us from losing money. They were wrong. Our first conference was very profitable as was the second, and the third, because there is an intensely hungry audience desirous of a more human, heart-to-heart, mutually respectful way of conducting commerce.

Persistence Paid Off

Today we have authored the first soft sell marketing book ever written. It reached the rank of number one in six amazon.com categories during our May 2009 launch. And we find ourselves with an international reputation as the leading voice for soft sell marketing.

We also founded the Soft Sell Marketers Association, a professional marketing association dedicated to training those who want to sell their valuable services but struggle with the whole idea of doing business. We show them who they really are and their value and lay out techniques by which they can make the income they desire without sacrificing their spiritual integrity.

And we produce our three-day Magnify Your Excellence trainings to help men and women get beyond the inner blocks that keep them stuck in place.

And none of this would have been possible without persistence. We were dedicated to that small and surprising voice that sent us off in the direction of marketing and selling, and through the dark days and nights, and there were quite a few, we kept to our vision, held to our course of action, endured what had to be endured, and here we are making an international contribution to life on this planet through *The Heart of Marketing*, demonstrating that love and commerce not only can go together, they must if we are to create a sustainable economy and infuse into the language of commerce a sense of dignity, spirituality, trust, and well-being that will make a better life for us all.

About Judith Sherven, PhD and Jim Sniechowski, PhD
Judith Sherven, PhD and Jim Sniechowski, PhD are a best selling husband and wife psychology team and the leading voice for soft sell, heart-based marketing. They produce the only Internet marketing conference for the soft sell community "Bridging Heart and Marketing. And their Soft Sell Marketers Association is an international hub for Soft Sell training and support. Their latest book is The Heart of Marketing: Love Your Customers and They Will Love You Back (Morgan James Publishing, May 2009) As guest experts they've been on over 1500 television and radio shows including Oprah, The View, 48 Hours, CNN, Canada AM, and The Daily Buzz. Judith & Jim are committed to bringing consciousness and conscience, caring and connection into the heart-beat of commerce around the world. And with that, Judith & Jim, we welcome you to the show.

Persistence By Robert Tuchman

Persistence. It is a word used to exemplify the never ending effort put forth by a pitcher trying to perfect his change up, a mother pushing her child to reach his highest potential, a student looking to get into her number one college, a marathon runner taking one step at a time, and an intern working his way up the corporate ladder. No matter who you are or what your profession is, persistence is everything—the only way to the top.

Let me share with you a story about a man whose persistence turned into success. This is Chris Shammas' story. Many years ago, I hired Chris as a salesperson and he became part of our hardworking team. When he first got started, things were not looking very promising for this young man; he was not where my company needed him to be and admittedly, I was seriously considering letting him go. I decided to speak to my partner Brett about Chris and get his input on the situation. Brett had talked me out of letting Chris go by explaining that he had seen something special in Chris and that I should give him another chance. Brett said,

"Look at him. Every time he gets beat down, he is able to pick himself off the mat and continue to go out there and get back in the fight. He always finds a new reason to start pounding the pavement again. Give him another chance."

And I did. Although things did not start picking up with Chris until the next year, when they did, the numbers were nothing short of amazing. His personal resolve—persistence, motivation and enthusiasm—was the number-one reason he succeeded and today, he is the top performing salesperson on our team of over thirty salespeople at Premiere Corporate Events, our company. I am convinced that because Chris never lost faith in himself, he was led to success. He would look around the room and say to himself, "Hey, if these other guys are making deals, why shouldn't I be doing the same thing and getting the same kinds of rewards?" Now, Chris is having a ball that is how it should be.

Chris' story is an inspiration to all of those trying to succeed at what they do. Be persistent! 'What goes around comes around'; I can't tell you how satisfying it is to prove this to yourself. When you can find a way to take the passion, energy, innocence, competitive spirit, and joy in yourself that you harnessed in order to achieve your goal, and you use that to help someone else reach his or her dream, you win the biggest victory of all: getting what you give.

As an entrepreneur myself, I have always said that the qualities that *always* make the difference between a business that succeeds and a business that fails is the persistence of the entrepreneur and their ability to bounce back from an obstacle. These two qualities, resilience and persistence, go hand-in-hand; it is impossible to succeed without either one of them.

When you are determined to turn your dream into a reality, it is vital to be persistent about *everything*, not just the big picture. Be persistent in asking yourself "Why not me?", "Why can't I be the best?", "Why not me to lead my company to success?" Persistently asking yourself stimulating questions such as these will help lead you to your ultimate goal, just as it led Chris to his. Know this: your energy, persistence, and commitment are far more important than your client list, or whether you've got a huge number of contacts, or how many years you've spent in the industry. You don't need twenty years of experience to act upon these qualities. It is better to utilize them sooner rather than later because these traits are contagious and you will be surprised how quickly you establish yourself as a player in whatever your endeavor may be.

There is a quote by Ray Kroc, creator of McDonalds, which I like to think about a lot when I am having a rough day in the office, things aren't going the way they should, and I think that there is nothing left to do but give up. Ray Kroc says,

"Nothing in the world can take the place of persistence. Talent will not; nothing is more common than unsuccessful men with talent. Genius will not; unrewarded genius is almost a proverb. Education alone will not; the world is full of educated derelicts. Persistence and determination alone are omnipotent."

Kroc's words are my everyday inspiration. I persistently reminding myself of this quote that in turn pushes me to constantly strive for bigger and better things, and until I reach these bigger and better achievements, I become relentless.

When I can take a moment out of my chaotic schedule to relax, I think about how I never could have imagined being in the position that I am in today, a successful entrepreneur. I am living my dream and I love every minute of it. I let my passion lead me to where I am now and I feel as though I am on top of the world. I credit all of my success to persistence, and I think Chris does too since it saved his career. I get up every morning ready to conquer the world, strive for the best, stay tough and be resilient, and always remember: Persistence is *everything*.

Focus on the Goal and Don't Give Up by Margo Berman

It seems like four years is my magic number. When I owned my ad agency, it took me four years to land any work with a global, credit card client. When I finally got a call, I went to a meeting and was told I had 24 hours to create an entire, multimedia campaign.

Would you call this formula for success: a four-year wait and a 24-hour opportunity? I did. My staff and I stayed up all night and created not one, but two bilingual campaigns. We won the business. The "Noche de Compras" (Night of Shopping) even drew thousands of people and became one of Puerto Rico's most successful events at a shopping center.

The fact is every obstacle has, at its core, the seeds of success. One of our clients, a mom-and-pop homemade chocolate store, was hard to find. It was hidden behind trees and a telephone pole. It was even tucked away on a side street. Customers would mistakenly go to its competitor, a few blocks away on the main street. One day, the owners discovered that the telephone pole obstructing their storefront was painted like a giant, red-and-white striped candy cane. No one had trouble finding it now. It took the city at least three months to repaint the pole. When asked if we had anything do to with it, of course we said, "It's illegal to paint city property," and smiled.

Another client was opening a new housing development. The problem was there wasn't any landscaping. How can you have a Grand Opening without any grass, trees, or foliage? The houses were sitting on dirt lots and were not very appealing. So, our agency created print ads and giant signs that said, "Catch us with our plants down! And save $2,000!" The Grand Opening was packed and they sold many houses. With a landscaping allowance, people could create the look they wanted.

The point is: Don't let obstacles become roadblocks. Persevere and find a way around them. After all, persistence is power. One of the most powerful quotes I ever read was by Winston Churchill. I typed it up, printed it out, and hung it in my office. Whenever people ask me why I never give up, I read this to them out loud:

Success is measured by your ability to maintain enthusiasm between failures.

I think every success I ever had was a result of not quitting. When I developed and hosted a radio show on public radio, I was the first to get a show sponsored. I was told, "Go get a sponsor." So I did. I wrote a proposal and sent it to several banks. One banker answered saying he was interested. When I went down to meet with him, he asked me what name should appear on the check. I called the station. All I heard was laughter in the background. It quickly became clear to me that the producer was joking when he told me to get a sponsor. The fact was that no one at this station had ever done this before. It took six weeks to find out to whom the check should be addressed.

I didn't know it couldn't be done. I just tried. I was like the bumblebee. It doesn't know its wings are short and its body is too fat to fly. It just flies.

Sometimes you can't listen to what others say. When someone says, "You can't do that!" I agree and say, "You're right. YOU can't do that." Just by changing the emphasis, you avoid defeatism and deflect negativity.

When someone says, "No," I hear, "Negotiation." And I continue my pursuit. It seems I've become rejection proof. I think of myself as having a Teflon coating. Rejection just slides off.

People often are frustrated because there is no evidence of any progress. They simply stop trying. What must happen, however, is to understand one three-letter word. A word that is nothing short of inspirational. What is it? It's the word "yet." Let me explain. When a mother has a child who is a slow developer and late to walk, and people ask her, "Why isn't she walking?" She simple responds: "She isn't walking YET!" Just the belief that her child will walk invites it to happen, replacing fear with expectation.

If we encourage people to approach all of their challenges like that and just add the word "yet" to every goal, just think how empowering that would be. They would be infused with belief and unwavering commitment to their most challenging goals.

For example, it took me four years to land my first book contract without the help of my literary agent. I called him my Secret Agent because no one ever knew what he was doing. I finally relieved him of his duty.

He started each conversation with: "The problem is..." Finally, I finished the sentence: "The problem is...YOU." I was determined to be that one in a thousand who gets a book deal. And I did. Not once. Not twice. But, now three times. This time, with one of the largest publishers in the world: John Wiley & Sons, the same company that has published more than 350 Nobel Laureates. Why? Because I refused to believe it wouldn't happen. No matter what I was told. And no matter how many times my manuscripts were rejected.

In fact, I had submitted several proposals to the same publisher, along with other publishing houses, that had been rejected. On the fourth year, one publisher asked me to write a proposal for a topic that wasn't my main area of expertise: design. I wrote the proposal. It was accepted. Then, I received a call telling me another editor not only accepted another proposal, but the book was finished. I received a copy of the manuscript and it followed my exact outline, chapter by chapter. This other author thought the same way I did.

So, I wrote another proposal on a topic in my area of expertise: advertising. The proposal was accepted with no changes and the publisher said, "Any other author would have given up on us." Not me, though. That proposal became my first book: *Street-Smart Advertising: How to Win the Battle of the Buzz*. It is now in the United Kingdom, India, and Russia (in Russian). I personally sent copies to book shows around the world, which is how it went global.

My second book, *The Brains Behind Great Ad Campaigns: Creative Collaboration between Copywriters and Art Directors*, is now available. I wrote it with the author who wrote the design book, exactly how I conceived it. We had two publishing offers and decided to stay with the publisher we both had: Rowman & Littlefield. We made a great team because, although we approach topics differently, our structural direction is similar.

Now, I'm writing my third book: *An Advertising Copywriter's Arsenal: A Guide to Writing Copy*. I had five publishing offers, resulting in a bidding war. I chose to go with Wiley & Sons, a prestigious house. Just by working diligently, creating quality work, and not giving up, now I'm pursued by publishers. What a difference a few years can make.

I'll leave you with a quote by Josh Billings I think makes my point best:

Consider the postage stamp. Its usefulness consists in the ability to stick to one thing till it gets there

About Margo Berman
Margo Berman is an award-winning advertising marketer and professor, as well as a Kauffman Faculty Scholar at Florida International University. Her first book, *Street-Smart Advertising: How to With the Battle of the Buzz*, is now in the UK, India, and Russia (in Russian). The two 6-CD award-winning webinar sets, based on the book, *Street-Smart Advertising* and *More Street-Smart Advertising*, won a national AWC Clarion Award for Educational Reference, She invented tactikPAK®, a patented system of learning, created Mental Peanut Butter® Training, and developed three advertising CDs. Her second book, *The Brains Behind Great Ad Campaigns*, explores the creative collaboration between copywriters and art directors. She's writing third advertising book, which examines all aspects of copywriting: *An Advertising Copywriter's Arsenal: A Guide to Writing Copy*. Her award-winning Web site exudes creativity www.UnlockTheBlock.com

The Path of Least Resistance by Carolyn Dean MD ND

Career choices are often based on guidance counseling in high school and can affect your whole life. According to Miss Elliot, my guidance counselor, my aptitude tests determined that I would make a wonderful nurse or executive secretary. I always got top marks, was vice president of the student council, a lead in the drama and dance clubs and on just about every other committee in the school. But, don't forget, this was the early 60's in Nova Scotia and I was a girl and girls didn't become doctors. I did go to university on a small scholarship to take BA Secretarial Science and only stayed long enough to learn typing and shorthand that have always served me well. Then I ran away from home with my boyfriend (and now husband of 40+ years) and in my travels became very interested in natural medicine.

Back home in Nova Scotia, I went back to university in honors biology and wondered about a career in ecology. I was dissuaded because on a summer job with the department of the environment I realized they didn't seem very focused on saving anything. A breakthrough came the day two friends in biology said they just got accepted into medicine. These two younger guys thought I was in premed and I realized that's exactly what I should be doing. I applied immediately.

At Dalhousie Medical School, in Halifax, Nova Scotia, third-year medical students are part of the interviewing process to accept new medical students. During my interview, I was asked if I thought I could make a difference in medicine. I said that I suspected I could and said I was interested in nutrition and lifestyle changes to help patients. A week later I was called in for an appointment with the Dean of Students, Dr. Fraser Nicholson, an open-minded psychiatrist and a true gentleman. He told me my third-year interview did not go well. The interviewers thought I would not make a good doctor. They felt I was naïve with a Pollyanna approach to medicine because I thought I could help people. Dr. Nicholson and I laughed!

If the third-year medical students that interviewed me had their way, I would never have set foot into medical school. I would probably never have trained in naturopathy, acupuncture, homeopathy, herbalism, nutrition, and Chinese medicine, all of which were invaluable tools in my medical practice, and continue to be priceless in my consulting and writing. I would never have developed an understanding of how natural medicine and allopathic medicine work and I would never have written a current total of eighteen books and developed a 48-week online wellness program called *Future Health Now*!

I realized later, as I went through the agonizing grind of medical school, that by third year, medical students are so beaten down by the system and have seen so many sick people in hospital-based settings, none of whom seemed to be getting "cured", that they know medicine is no place for a healer - and no place to get healed!

Fortunately, Dr. Nicholson said I had a good head on my shoulders, a sparkle in my eye, and a sharp wit, all of which would make me a very fine doctor. We both agreed that the third-year students had gotten it all wrong. Thankfully, their negative opinion of me was tossed out the window and didn't factor into my application or my acceptance into med school. And, as the fates would have it, Miss Elliot was now working in the Dean of Medicine's office and she was also on the medical acceptance committee! She realized she had guided me in the wrong direction and became a big fan of me getting into medicine.

That interview was in 1973, and idealism in medicine was a rare commodity. Also on the endangered list were nutrition, natural medicine, equality and ethics. I entered medicine with a view to educating people about nutrition and lifestyle but what I found was a pervasive indoctrination against anything not drug-oriented and surgery-oriented. In my first days of medical school we were repeatedly warned against chiropractors, herbalists, and health faddists. Making my own yogurt and eating it during breaks made me a subject of derision among my classmates, which only ended when Dr. Nicholson asked me for my recipe in front of my class!

The three main battles I had in medicine were the "boys club", lack of ethics training and lack of nutrition education and here's how I overcame them.

The Naughty Boys Club
In the very first week of medical school, one of the introductory instructors spiced up his talk with slides of nude females from *Playboy Magazine*. It was obvious this was 'standard operating procedure' at Dalhousie and I was shocked and outraged. I could see that the other women in the class were similarly horrified. What could we do? We muttered under our breaths and most of the men just laughed, albeit somewhat nervously.

I didn't know anyone in the class yet. When I applied for medical school I learned that Dalhousie usually admitted twenty-five women in a class of 100. My class overcame that barrier by accepting thirty-three women. Even so, we were outnumbered but I knew something had to be done.

Playgirl Magazine had just hit the stands in 1973. I

bought the latest copy at the local drug store amidst the stares. I only had two days before that lecturer was back and I had to work fast. I convinced a medical professor friend to make me some nude male slides at the university. Miraculously, he got them back to me the next day. He had a wicked sense of humor and I think he wanted to see the proverbial dung hit the fan.

Telling no one my plan, minutes before class, I inserted the nude slides in the chauvinist lecturer's slide carousel and waited for the explosion. My heart was pounding from the excitement and anticipation. The lights went down, a gorgeous hunk in his birthday suit filled up the screen and the class went hysterical. The women hooted, the men howled. We laughed together and we all bonded as the fumbling professor tried to regain his composure and his slides as he unceremoniously exited the class.

We actually never saw him again and we never saw another nude female slide from anyone else the whole year. I was told that similarly "insensitive" pictures were immediately taken down all over the medical campus. That one simple act leveled the playing field with no protests, no whining and complaining, no letters of protest to the school medical board, no hunger strikes and no marches. Just Direct Action.

Lack of Ethics Training in Medicine
A fellow medical student and I recognized a huge gap in our education and we started an Ethics Club. Inconceivably, there were no ethics courses in our medical education program. Young medical students, some as young as 19, with only two years of undergraduate training, are thrown into the world of life and death medicine without any survival skills for themselves or for their future patients. They live a very

abnormal life of massive stress and study for six to eight years after which they are expected to go out into the world and act as if they know all there is to know about the human body, mind, and spirit. In fact, we were told many times that if we didn't learn it in medical school it must be quackery! So, we were expected to know it all.

Instead of asking the administration to organize an ethics course, which we knew would take years to implement, we started renting mail-order ethics films to be shown once a week. At our noon-hour ethics meetings we viewed and then discussed life and death questions facing burn victims, cancer survivors, and depressed patients. Our ethics club, besides helping students cope, had another welcome outcome. It embarrassed the administration into forming an ethics course in the following years.

Nutrition and Lifestyle Medicine
This was not something I was able to influence in medical school. However, I've spent the last 30 years developing a way to get this information to the public in a usable form.

There are no nutrition classes in school there is no nutrition training given to doctors. Where are people supposed to obtain this vital information? Certainly they aren't getting it from the TV ads that promote highly processed synthetic food and reinforce television and computer culture. Even the current trend toward what I call "celebrity" supplements doesn't emphasize diet, exercise and lifestyle. Unless someone is making money on a product, you'll never see the promotion of basic healthy habits in our society.

That's why I persisted in my study of natural medicine and in 2009 produced a 48-week online wellness program called *Future Health Now*! My gift to you is a free first week module. I encourage you to become a member and get healthy. Health happens to people who make the choice to be healthy and I've got the tools for you.

Meet The Doctor of the Future: Dr. Dean is a medical doctor, naturopath, herbalist and acupuncturist with a busy telephone consulting practice. She's authored and co-authored 18 books including the Magnesium Miracle, The Yeast Connection and Women's Health, IBS for Dummies and IBS Cookbook for Dummies. She's also the medical director of the Nutritional Magnesium Association. You're invited to join her 48-week online wellness program Future Health Now! Receive the first module free at www.drcarolyndean.com/futurehealthnow and a free subscription to her Doctor of the Future newsletter.

A Financially Literate Society is Worth the Choice! By Elisabeth Donati

Many years ago the Universe handed me an idea on a silver platter and requested that I run with it. Actually, it all started when I asked myself this question, "Why doesn't someone create a summer camp for children and teens where they can learn all of the information I wished I'd learned about money and investing when I was young?"

I wasn't thinking that I would be the one to do it except that, when you ask these types of questions, the obvious reply often suggests doing it yourself. Well, that's exactly what I did. I took it upon myself to create the finest financial literacy program on the face of the planet. That program is now called Camp Millionaire and it teaches and empowers the adults of tomorrow how to make, manage and multiply their money wisely, while doing good in the world. And it does so in a playful, life-simulated environment with a curriculum where the kids are the "pieces" of a game they play called The Money Game.

In the beginning, my thought was to produce a single summer camp called The Money Camp for Kids. "How hard can this be?" I asked myself. Simply write a curriculum, schedule a facility, market the camp and teach it. At least that was the initial idea.

If you've ever heard the concept of the three realms of knowledge: the stuff you know you know, the stuff you know you don't know and the stuff you don't know you don't know, you might have already guessed that I had just stepped into the biggest puddle of stuff I didn't know I didn't know. I breathed in deeply and stepped into a new financial paradigm to teach kids about money; and more importantly, teach them how to think differently about money.

That first camp in 2002 had 39 amazing kids in it, ages 9 to 15, and when I realized that the knowledge they gained in that one program could set them up for powerful, successful lives, I couldn't stop. Parents asked me when I was going to do another camp. Adults asked me to teach them the same information I was teaching the kids. People from all over the world wanted me to teach them what I was doing so they could teach the program in their own communities. There was no going back. I had started something bigger than myself and the idea of NOT doing it didn't even occur to me. It was simply not an option. I felt that then and I still feel that way today.

Actually, in 2002, one of the original members of my board of directors told me in no uncertain terms, "If you knew what it was going to take to create a real business out of this fabulous idea of yours, you would run away right now and hide." I sensed that he was probably right. But even so, I thought, how can I stop the growth that happens now I have given birth to an idea that everyone in the world thinks is important, worthy and necessary? It turns out we were both right. I didn't have any idea what it would take and, now that I'm in it, I couldn't run away and hide if I wanted to. Why?

There's one thing that keeps me going each day...when I'm tired of sitting in front of the computer and my fingers are exhausted from answering emails. When I'm overwhelmed with the details of organizing people and numbers and paper, and frustrated with the constant need to find funding to grow this venture into the adult company it's beginning to be.

What keeps me moving forward every day, whether I want to or not, is a trait called persistence. In the face of difficulty, opposition or exhaustion, my firm commitment to being the type of person who sets a powerful example of persistence keeps me putting one foot in front of the other, no matter what might try to get in my way.

In amongst the piles of papers and to-do lists, taped to a black, plastic envelope holder, is an old worn playing card-sized piece of cardstock with a photo of a tree-covered mountainside sitting resolutely behind a poem that was written by Marilyn Wilson. This poem is a constant reminder for me when the days are long, when it doesn't feel like I've made any progress or when people seem to be asking for more and more of me.

The poem is entitled, "Don't Quit." If you've never read it before, it goes like this:

When things go wrong, as they sometimes will,
when the road you're trudging seems all uphill,
when the funds are low and the debts are high,
and you want to smile, but you have to sigh,
when care is pressing you down a bit,
rest if you must, but Don't You Quit!
Life is odd with its twists and turns,
as everyone of us sometimes learns,
and many a failure turns about,
when he might have won had he stuck it out.
Don't give up though the pace seems slow,
you may succeed with another blow.
Often the goal is nearer than
it seems to a faint and faltering man.
Often the struggler has given up,
when he might have captured the victor's cup.
And he learned too late when the night came down,
how close he was to the golden crown.

Success is failure turned inside out.
The silver tint of the clouds of doubt.
And you never can tell how close you are.
It may be near when it seems so far.
So stick to the fight when you're hardest hit.
It's when things seem the worst that you must not quit!

Persistence can be misunderstood. It's important to note that persistence doesn't always mean, "choosing not to quit." There are a couple of distinctions and a state of mind that will help explain. You see, there is a difference between giving up (or quitting) because you think you can't go on and giving up because you don't know what else to do. There's a difference between being persistent because you have utter faith in the outcome and vision versus sticking with it because you don't want to "fail".

Persistence is the trait that has you move past the unknowns, has you rely on your faith in yourself and tap into your ability to see beyond the immediate reality.

There is a common saying originally coined by Vincent Thomas "Vince" Lombardi. "Winners never quit and quitters never win." Most people buy this saying hook, line and sinker. Though there is some obvious truth to this, if you listen to it within the realm of business, a flaw becomes visible.

Successful business people "quit" all the time. The thing is, they know when to quit. They have the wisdom and experience to know the difference between quitting because something isn't going to work, no matter how good the initial idea, and giving up simply because they lack the fortitude to do what it takes to bring a dream to fruition. Smart business people know that choosing to quit is sometimes the smartest and best decision to make. And here's where the state of mind comes into play. They don't define it as giving up or failing. They make their assessment, make the call and reapply their passion and experience to their next vision and goal.

What keeps persistence alive in me when many others would have tossed in the towel are the continual calls and emails I receive from overjoyed parents who send their kids to my programs, women whose lives are touched by the simple directive to Pay Yourself First, parents who read The Ultimate Allowance and finally have a way to provide their children with the necessary financial experience to grow into money savvy adults. When the work I do each day improves the experience people have on this planet, it ceases being 'work' and becomes who I am. It drives me because I no longer need to drive it.

The ability to be persistent is a gift. I believe we all have it from birth. Using or not using it is a choice. And, until further notice, I will choose persistence.

About Elisabeth Donati

Elisabeth Donati's passion is empowering others to be responsible for themselves and the world. She is the owner of Creative Wealth Intl., LLC and creator of Camp Millionaire, a unique financial intelligence program for kids and teens. Her other passions include her new Creative Wealth for Women and Celebrating Women & Wealth workshops designed for the special financial needs of women. Elisabeth is an expert in teaching the basic financial principles everyone need in a way that is engaging, empowering and fun. She is the author of the financial parenting book, The Ultimate Allowance and publishes her own weekly Ezine, Financial Wisdom with a TWI$T!

"You are never given a wish
without also being given the
power to make it true. You may
have to work for it, however."
~Richard Bach

Justin Sachs Coaching is designed to empower you with the focus, training and accountability you need to achieve the consistent results you demand in the most important areas of your life. Just as a personal fitness trainer helps you raise your standards for accelerated results in your body, your Justin Sachs Coach will challenge and support you in attaining the results you desire and deserve. Focus is power. The first step will be for you and your coach to truly define with clarity the results you are committed to achieving. Next, you will assess, with absolute candor, where you are right now and where you want to be – and what's in between. Your coach will help identify the things that keep you from achieving the results you desire and deserve – and then work with you to create a game plan. It is not based on hope. It is not based on theory. It is modeled after those who have already achieved real results. You will work with a highly skilled coach selected to closely match your individual needs. You will take massive, intelligent action to achieve your goals. Your coach will empower you by holding you accountable to the commitments you make. Your coach will help measure, monitor and manage your progress, and along the way support you to take consistent action that leads to the results you demand. You are about to enter a partnership that will change your life. We take that responsibility seriously – and we deliver.

For More Information visit www.JustinSachsCoaching.com

About the Author - Justin Sachs

Entrepreneur and Executive Leadership Coach, Wellness Expert, and Best-selling Personal Development Author

Justin Sachs is a six-year coaching veteran and has honed his skills as a wellness expert, having worked with individuals ranging from those who are severely depressed to those who are looking to take their lives the next level.

Projects and Foundations

- Best-selling Author of teen guidebook *Your Mailbox Is Full-Real Teens in the Real World* created to equip today's youth with the life-skills and leadership principles necessary for a full, successful life
- Founder and Chairman of Peak Performance Lifestyles Foundation, a non-profit organization dedicated to empowering teenagers with the tools they need to become leaders and contributors to their communities
- Founder of Motivational Minds Radio Network, a one-of-a-kind inspirational talk show network that brings together the greatest personalities in Personal and Business Development
- Founder of the Teen Development Awards dedicated to recognizing the greatest in youth leadership and teen development products

Through his tireless efforts in community awareness, teen development and active leadership, Justin Sachs plays a pivotal role in the formation of an enriched society. A strong advocate of cultural diversity, strides towards inner wellness, entrepreneurism and youth empowerment, Justin is a powerful speaker with an even more powerful message.

For more information on Justin Sachs visit his website at www.JSachs.com or call 888-357-4441.

LaVergne, TN USA
06 December 2009
166133LV00004B/4/P

9 780982 575505